Praise for *Re...*

In *Required*, Claude Alexander an... ...the transformative power of cross-cult... ...posure, cultural translation, and a passion for Christ-mandated conciliation and unity. With great transparency, they urge us to reflect on how our racial story connects to His Story and mission of reconciling our diverse world to Himself and each other.

—DR. BARBARA WILLIAMS-SKINNER
Co-Convener, National African American Clergy Network

Mac and Claude are two extraordinary men whom I admire deeply. Their work to advance racial justice and advocate for city transformation has been stellar. This book serves as both inspirational and a framework for advancing the gospel and overcoming racial division.

—BRYAN L. CARTER
Senior pastor, Concord Baptist Church, Dallas, TX

From 1938–1940 the Swedish economist (later Noble Laureate 1974) Gunnar Myrdal made a two-year study tour of the USA to investigate the issue of economic inequality and racial division in America. Myrdal saw a direct link between racial inequality, poverty among African Americans, and a threat to American democracy. Seven decades later that dilemma is as real as ever. This book teaches, guides, and propels us toward God's design of racial reconciliation while highlighting the role of relationships and movements such as the Lausanne Movement and Movement.org in bridging the divide. A timely and challenging reminder that racial equality and racial justice are required of those who belong to God's new kingdom.

—LAS G. NEWMAN, PH.D.
Global Associate Director for Regions, Lausanne Movement

My two good friends have collaborated to write this book that, given their respective backgrounds and friendship, speaks powerfully into the call on each of us to practice justice, mercy, and humility to overcome racial tensions.

—Bob Doll
Chief investment officer, Crossmark Global Investments

In *Required*, two internationally respected Christian leaders allow us to "overhear" them as they have the kind of conversation many wish they could have: honest, direct, vulnerable, reasonable, and full of love. This book will equip the reader with a path toward seeking justice and mercy, as followers of Jesus are called to do, and to standing with and for one another, as brothers and sisters must.

—Russell Moore
Christianity Today

In a world where racial conversations are fraught with blame, shame, language landmines, and implicit and explicit assumptions of guilt and responsibility, we long for examples of ways forward. Told through a beautiful tapestry of mentoring, courage, humility, family, pain, grace, and guts, Alexander and Pier provide a story that informs and enlarges our story.

—Steve Moore
CEO, Murdock Trust

Claude and Mac are heroes to cities and city movements. They are doing really impressive work that sets the foundational concepts to enable people to flourish and organizations around the world to thrive.

—Scott Beck
CEO and entrepreneur

Amid all the noise surrounding the discussion and debate about race in America, *Required* is essential reading. Not only does it root the conversation in Scripture, it individualizes the process people can take to be a positive presence in what needs to be done.

—Darrell Bock
Executive director for cultural engagement, Howard G. Hendricks Center for Christian Leadership and Cultural Engagement; senior research professor of New Testament studies, Dallas Theological Seminary

Bishop Claude Alexander is a man who has led at the forefront of Christ-centered racial reconciliation for decades. He and his good friend Mac Pier not only inform us, but they call us to act. My prayer is that readers of this book will be inspired to a more faithful pursuit of following Jesus by loving their neighbors well.

—CASEY CRAWFORD
CEO, Movement Mortgage

Bishop Claude Alexander and Dr. Mac Pier come together to write a compelling narrative of the roots, present realities, and future hope for a racially divided world. *Required* should be required reading for all who call themselves children of the Most High God.

—REV. ADAM DURSO, D.D.
President, LEAD.NYC, vice president, Movement.org;
NYC mayor's Clergy Advisory Council

Through biblical imperatives and their own testimonies, Alexander and Pier detail a spiritual and practical path toward racial unity. Their two very different origins converge under one cross and one call, beautifully challenging the church to dismantle racial division through justice, mercy, and humility.

—JUSTIN E. GIBONEY
President, The AND Campaign

Mac Pier and Claude Alexander use their experiences to give us a blueprint and a way forward for racial healing in this nation. A must read for all who seek a unified nation free of racial conflict.

—THE HONORABLE REV. DR. W. WILSON GOODE, SR.
Former mayor, City of Philadelphia

In this wise and compelling work, Claude Alexander and Mac Pier show that what is required of Christians is also essential for understanding our fraught and racially fragmented times, and embarking on a new path. Their stories illuminate the injustice and incomprehension that has divided those within as well as outside the church and show the ways in which that requirement to seek, love, and practice justice, mercy, and humility can bring hope and healing to a riven land.

—CHERIE HARDER
President, The Trinity Forum

I've heard the question asked recently, "What do we do in times like these?" In *Required*, Claude Alexander and Mac Pier provide practical wisdom to help answer this question while echoing the message of Scripture—love God and love others. This book encourages and motivates us to action by reminding us that change occurs as we live according to God's call.

—J. FRANK HARRISON III
Chairman & CEO, Coca-Cola Consolidated

Since prejudice is everyone's problem, reconciliation must be everyone's responsibility. *Required* practically helps you take your place as a reconciler. I highly recommend it.

—DAVID D. IRELAND, PH.D.
Lead pastor, Christ Church, northern New Jersey;
author of *Raising a Child Who Prays*

Bishop Claude Alexander and Dr. Mac Pier are two leaders I highly respect. I encourage you to read this book during these challenging times in our country.

—JOHN K. JENKINS, SR.
Senior pastor, First Baptist Church of Glenarden, Maryland

You cannot walk away from this book without a disruption in your soul, compelled to live differently to usher in a more equitable future that is mutually flourishing for all.

—LISA JERNIGAN
Co-founder and president, Amplify Peace

Claude and Mac exude the fragrance of Jesus. They walk their talk. Their thoughtful book provides a succinct yet thorough look at racism today and then engagingly gives pathways forward for practical life-transforming change. They can help us, the readers, respond with increased wisdom and potency, for such a time as this.

—CHERYL MEREDITH KRUEGER, PHD
Chief Ideation Officer, Navigator Workplace

Grounded in their own testimonies of transformation and inspiring initiatives that are impacting our cities, Pier and Alexander equip us to pursue God's call to overcome racial division in both our personal lives and in our communities.

—Tom Lin
President and CEO, InterVarsity Christian Fellowship

Overcoming division is personal for Claude and Mac and has been their lifelong work. They invite us into their story and provide a clear map to racial healing.

—Jim Liske
US executive director, Movement.org

There is much written today on racial healing, but Claude Alexander and Mac Pier powerfully pinpoint the pathway through *Required*. The writing is compelling through the venues of personal experience, biblical exposition, systemic racism history, yet an underlying hope for change. There is space for repentance and a fresh look at the power of the gospel for healing. Frankly, this is *the* book for these days for the church to move forward and lead as God intended.

—Jo Anne Lyon
General Superintendent Emerita, The Wesleyan Church

Through their friendship and ministry partnership, Dr. Mac Pier and Bishop Claude Alexander have created a meaningful framework of what it looks like to live better together. They remind us that racial healing begins with the sharing of our stories. An important book for important times!

—Rev. Dr. Nicole Martin
Senior Vice President of Ministry Impact, American Bible Society

As a reporter and interviewer, I love books that take me on a journey and this one did. Claude and Mac have lived, and more importantly journeyed, together when it comes to the issue of race. Claude and Mac get it!

—Maina Mwaura
Consultant at mainaspeaks.com;
author, Howard Hendricks biography; missions pastor

Required is an urgent pivot in the tired dialogue on race among evangelicals, which too often is an end in itself, devoid of missional context. For this generation, which roots personal reconciliation and systemic racial justice as core to the human narrative, *Required* will help Christian leaders embrace a new and much needed path.

—R. YORK MOORE
Executive director, Catalytic Partnerships, InterVarsity
West Ridge Church, Dallas, Georgia

During this kairos hour, God is calling the church to move toward racial justice and equity. In *Required*, Claude Alexander and Mac Pier seek God's heart to be conduits of biblically-based healing. The call is for the faith community to understand our history as we prayerfully rise up and press forward to be God's shining light.

—BARBARA L. PEACOCK, D. MIN
Chair, biblical studies, Chun University;
author of *Soul Care in African-American Practice*

Mac and Claude are right: We don't choose our race but we choose if we obey God's requirements. Thanks to their personal authenticity, their powerful scriptural analysis, and their practical ideas, I believe God will use this book as rocket fuel for your racial journey and pursuit of racial justice.

—KARA POWELL, PhD
Chief of leadership formation for Fuller Seminary;
executive director of the Fuller Youth Institute; coauthor
of *Three Big Questions that Change Every Teenager*

It is required of every one of us—every child of God—that we think biblically, talk honestly, and act lovingly with regard to ethnic diversity and racial unity in the church and in our culture. There is no one I trust more to guide me on these subjects than Claude Alexander. In *Required*, Bishop Alexander—together with his colleague Dr. Mac Pier—shares his life experiences with racial division and teaches us the requisite biblical virtues for us to become agents of reconciliation.

—PHILIP RYKEN
President, Wheaton College

Required is a distinct call to action rooted in an understanding of Scripture and ourselves. Using their personal stories as a backdrop, Claude and Mac compellingly invite us to reach beyond our "own limits" to live into the beauty—and challenge—of Jesus' call to unity.

—CRAIG SIDER
President and CEO, Movement.org

This important, timely book points the way to the future God desires. *Required*'s two authors—one White, one Black—have been dramatically successful for decades in interracial dialogue and cooperation. This significant work shows us how we all can join them in promoting the church and society that the God of justice demands.

—RONALD J. SIDER
Distinguished professor emeritus of theology,
holistic ministry, and public policy,
Palmer Seminary at Eastern University

Claude and Mac model for us how our faith should inform both our public and private witness—a witness that can rally your sphere of influence towards the opportunities of divine redemption. I marvel at how they were planted by God in families and communities which shaped their world view and birthed their platforms of leadership. It's through their example that we are challenged to sacrificially pursue the call of God to serve as conduits of healing.

—REV. EBONY SMALL
Vice President of Global Ministries,
Pulse Movement

This book is a constructive apologetic for reconciliation in Christ—culturally, socially, and personally. What drives this book and what should motivate Christians globally to make this a priority is the following sentence from the book: "The church of Jesus Christ is required to work at a level of unity as never experienced before to make a redemptive difference in the world."

—DR. SCOTT SUNDQUIST
President, Gordon Conwell Seminary

Bishop Claude Alexander and Dr. Mac Pier have given us a glimpse of their own personal journeys and why we have to look at the problems of justice and race through the microscope and not the telescope. I encourage those who want to honestly face the horrors of racism—this social malignancy that has been a part of the fabric of our continuing experience—to dive into this book through their own experience and feel the grace that this work offers.

—BISHOP WALTER THOMAS
Pastor, New Psalmist Baptist Church;
presiding prelate, The Kingdom Association of Covenant Pastors

For nearly a decade, I have had the privilege of watching and working with Claude Alexander and Mac Pier as they have confronted the most disruptive barriers to racial equity and justice in our cities and across our nation. This book is a gift to us all and will help you find your place as a part of the solution to the divide that continues as a barrier to the advancement of the gospel.

—DR. JEFF WARREN
Senior pastor, Park Cities Baptist Church, Dallas, Texas

I have known Bishop Claude Alexander and Dr. Mac Pier for more than a decade. I trust them for many reasons, including their thoughtfulness, their accomplishments, and their track record. I trust them most of all because of their long record of faithfulness and commitment to Jesus. We need trusted people who have labored and led for the long haul to help us understand where we've been and where we need to go, particularly on issues of race and racial justice.

—MICHAEL WEAR
Author of *Reclaiming Hope*;
coauthor of *Compassion & Conviction*

In *Required*, Claude Alexander and Mac Pier have given us a gift. They've invited us into their honest, meaningful, and theologically rich conversation about gospel integrity and racial reconciliation. In a deeply divided time, Alexander and Pier are healers of the breach.

—PETER WEHNER
Senior fellow, Ethics and Public Policy Center,
contributing opinion writer, the *New York Times*,
contributing writer, *The Atlantic*

REQUIRED

God's Call to
Justice, Mercy,
and Humility
to Overcome
Racial Division

CLAUDE ALEXANDER
MAC PIER

Movement Day Publishing
New York City

Movement Day Publishing is the publishing ministry of Movement. org, an organization that catalyzes leaders in more than one hundred cities to see their cities flourish spiritually and socially. Movement.org trains leaders globally to create their own Movement Day Expressions. For more information, visit movement.org.

REQUIRED: God's Call to Justice, Mercy, and Humility to Overcome Racial Division

© 2021 by Claude Alexander and Mac Pier

A Movement Day resource published in alliance with Movement.org.

All rights reserved. No part of this book may be reproduced in any form without permission in writing from the publisher, except in the case of brief quotations embodied in critical articles or reviews.

All Scripture quotations, unless otherwise indicated, are taken from the Holy Bible, New International Version®, NIV®. Copyright © 1973, 1978, 1984, 2011 by Biblica, Inc.™ Used by permission of Zondervan. All rights reserved worldwide. www.zondervan.com. The "NIV" and "New International Version" are trademarks registered in the United States Patent and Trademark Office by Biblica, Inc.™ Scripture quotations marked (ESV) are from the ESV® Bible (The Holy Bible, English Standard Version®), copyright © 2001 by Crossway, a publishing ministry of Good News Publishers. Used by permission. All rights reserved. Scripture quotations marked KJV are taken from the King James Version. Scripture quotations marked (NLT) are taken from the Holy Bible, New Living Translation, copyright ©1996, 2004, 2015 by Tyndale House Foundation. Used by permission of Tyndale House Publishers, a Division of Tyndale House Ministries, Carol Stream, Illinois 60188. All rights reserved.

Edited by Ginger Kolbaba
Cover by Yvonne Parks at pearcreative.ca
Interior by Katherine Lloyd at theDESKonline.com
Cataloging-in-Publication Data is available.

ISBN 978-1-7324353-6-0 (print)
ISBN 978-1-7324353-7-7 (e-book)
ISBN 978-1-7324353-8-4 (audio book)

Printed in the United States of America

21 22 23 24 25 5 4 3 2 1

To Roderick and Beverly Caesar for their generosity.

To Mayor Wilson Goode for his friendship,
and to Gary and Lynette Frost for their heroism.

To William Avalon, Dianne English, and Ivan Hinrichs
whose friendship, commitment, courage, and support
have been sources of light and lift.

CONTENTS

FOREWORD

I got married on June 19, 2004. I chose that date because I wanted to get married as soon as I graduated from undergrad in order to start my new life with my then-fiancée. It was the earliest date available at my selected venue after my May 2 graduation, so I signed on the dotted line and started planning the affair. I had so many details to attend to and I was wholly unprepared. I had never attended a wedding before, so I had no point of reference for what its planning required, but as the day approached, I got more and more excited.

The week of my wedding I remember seeing a television commercial about a Juneteenth festival happening that day, but since I did not know what Juneteenth was, I shrugged my shoulders and let that detail slip through the cracks of my mind. Our wedding day came, and it was as beautiful and exciting as I had imagined it would be. My grandfather walked me down the aisle in the place of my father who had passed away shortly before my second birthday. My husband and I exchanged vows and cut our cake with family and friends smiling in our direction. June 19th would be our wedding anniversary. An annual reminder of the day we became one.

It was not until a decade later that I learned our wedding anniversary had more significance than the date our venue was available. I, a then-thirty-one-year-old Black American woman, learned that, after thirteen years of public school, four years of undergraduate studies, and two years of graduate school, I had never heard of or learned what Juneteenth was. As a matter of fact, my understanding of the history of my people in America was that they were slaves, but President Abraham Lincoln emancipated them after the Civil War, and the Civil Rights Movement helped secure the full rights and privileges of Black Americans. The end.

I learned that Juneteenth represented a two-year delay in the news of emancipation reaching slaves in Texas, but as my knowledge became fuller through the years, I came to understand that even that framing was wrong. It was not that, somehow, maybe due to lack of technology or the time it took for news to travel from Washington, DC, to Texas, slaves simply did not hear about their emancipation between 1863 and 1865. No. Juneteenth represents two years that Confederate soldiers and slaveowners actively terrorized the enslaved and denied them access to the rights of emancipation until the Union Army showed up.

Many Christ followers are calling for racial unity in this nation and in the church. But unity always and necessarily requires acknowledging the truth with humility first. The humility to wrestle with a truth that hurts. The humility to wrestle with a truth that even shames. The humility to wrestle with a truth that leads to prayer. The humility to wrestle with a truth that leads to repentance. As we examine what is required for racial unity, let us remember that the first tactic Satan uses to create disunity is to distort truth. He did it in the garden of Eden and is doing it today. My hope is that we will be called back to truth through the powerful and prophetic words of this book—a book Bishop Claude Alexander and Dr. Mac Pier have lovingly penned with the goal of ushering us back to the truth that leads to humility, prayer, and repentance, according to 2 Chronicles 7:14—to the truth that heals.

Thirty percent of Americans identify as Republican. Thirty-one percent of Americans identify as Democrat. But 65 percent of Americans identify as Christian—more than both major political parties combined. We are not waiting on Congress to fix what is broken, we are waiting on the church. It is time for us to be the change we wish to see in America. This is what is required, and it is our reasonable service.

—*Nona Jones*
Founder, Faith & Prejudice; head of Faith Global, Facebook

ADDRESSING THE VERY REAL RACIAL TENSION

In a March 2021 Gallup poll questioning how much Americans personally worried about race relations, 73 percent said they worried a great deal or fair amount. Seventy-one percent expressed being either very dissatisfied or somewhat dissatisfied with the state of race relations.[1]

A July 6, 2021, release of an InterVarsity Christian Fellowship survey of student attitudes on 127 campuses revealed that their most important social issue is racial justice (39 percent).[2]

In a June 17, 2020, posting, "Barna's Perspective on Race and the Church," Barna president David Kinnaman wrote:

The past few weeks have been a time of listening, learning, repentance and lament for the Barna team. As social researchers who seek to equip the Church to effectively engage with the world, we find ourselves standing alongside other believers in an effort to right the wrongs of racial injustice. As a team, we have begun with deep soul searching. About how we have contributed to problems of racial inequity, whether implicitly or explicitly. About how we can better listen to and serve our Black and brown brothers and sisters in Christ.

This soul searching is more than a few days or weeks of processing and then getting back to business as usual. We commit ourselves to both short-term actions and long-term results as we seek to be a catalyst for genuine and lasting change in the Church.[3]

No attempt to be the church of Jesus Christ in America can occur without addressing the very real racial tension within her as a result of the historical and contemporary realities of racism. These tensions exist not only within America, but also within the church. In a September 1, 2020, Barna article, "Race Today: How the Summer of 2020 Changed Perceptions of Racial Justice—and What It Means for Church Leaders," when researchers asked the general population, "Do you think our country has a race problem?" Thirty-seven percent of Whites, 76 percent of Blacks, and 58 percent of Hispanics said definitely. The numbers of self-identifying Christians is even more telling with 33 percent of Whites, 81 percent of Blacks, and 56 percent of Hispanics saying definitely. Barna was unable to report on Asians because of the low sample size.[4] The gap in perception and perspective is one that presents a significant challenge to the church's witness both in the United States and around the world.

This has been a point of profound concern for the two of us. I (Claude) am a Black pastor of The Park Church in Charlotte, North Carolina. Mac is a White prayer movement leader and founder of Movement.Org, a global city movement organization. Mac is also the Lausanne co-catalyst for cities.

Over the past five years, our relationship and partnership in the gospel has come to terms with the critical need for the church to positively engage the subject of racism in America from the perspective of the claims of God as revealed in the Bible and a knowledge of history. The following is the fruit of that growth in honesty, transparency, understanding, acceptance, and continued commitment. It is written from the perspective of two Christians whose calling to the church and to the cities of the world compels us to address difficult and painful realities, assured of God's power to redeem and to reconcile. We write this to and for the church as well as for those who desire to see the church be an agent of human flourishing.

Defining racism is as difficult as it is important. In fact I (Mac) believe we need the help of others to identify racist perspectives that we may hold. This requires candor and courage. I view racism as holding a view of racial superiority over other races, whether privately or corporately. In this book Claude does a masterful job of providing the historical context for the conversation of race. Just as I as a White person have needed Claude's historical analysis to help me grasp corporate racism, we need each other to wrestle with, learn from, and become truth tellers to each other.

And for me (Claude), racism is the denial, frustration, and antagonism of the personhood, place, and/or participation of an individual or group due to race. Racist acts deny, antagonize, or frustrate a person or group's dignity and value, right to belong, and to fully participate as an equal. Racist attitudes ascribe or demonstrate negative and low value toward individuals and groups based upon race.

The bottom line is that we are incomplete without each other on this journey toward overcoming racial division.

This book hinges on two fundamental beliefs. The first is that God calls us to address racial tensions in His call "to do justice, love mercy, and walk humbly before our God" (Micah 6:8). The second is that the process of addressing the tensions and the realities underlying them requires awareness, ownership, and agency.

Having found that the pursuit of such an effort necessitates truly knowing ourselves, one another, and our collective history, chapters 1 and 2 begin with our individual stories, followed by chapter 3, in which we offer a reflection of our relational story. With chapter 4, I (Claude) provide an exposition of Micah 6:1-8. Then we divide chapters 5 through 12 into three sectional pairings—awareness with humility, ownership with mercy, and agency with justice. The alert reader will note that these pairings are not aligned to the order of mention in the scriptural passage, but according to the process we are suggesting, being that of awareness, ownership, and agency. We believe that awareness creates humility, that mercy prompts ownership, and that agency promotes the doing of justice. Within these sections, we present a biblical exposition, followed by a case study of how the pairings are pursued. We also include a summary of the history of race in America, as well as we address certain elephants in the room. In chapter 13, we provide suggestions for what's next.

Our desire in *Required* is to think carefully and conscientiously about our personal and collective racial journeys. These journeys are intended to shape our discipleship, including the depth of our love for those different from us. We invite you to enter into Jesus' concern for God's *shalom* for all people. His call on our lives is to passionately pursue His vision for a church that is united, compassionate, and muscular in bringing His kingdom to earth. We are never more like Jesus than when we radically love those who are radically different from us.

A united church in a racially divided world is the Great Antidote to bring God's love and pragmatic solutions to racial and ethnic brokenness. May we grow in Christlikeness. As He gave Himself for the whole world, He invites us to do the same.

Chapter 1

ORIGINS IN BLACK AND WHITE: CLAUDE'S STORY

Answering God's call to overcome racial division has not been a matter of choice for me. Being born an African-American male in 1964 made this vocation unavoidable. The families into which I was born have unique histories.

My maternal grandfather, Carl Que Hickerson Sr., was a second-generation Baptist pastor from Oklahoma who served churches in several cities across the US, including Washington, DC, where my mother grew up. In the course of his pastorate there, he was among a host of pastors with whom President Truman met concerning the desegregation of the military. My maternal grandmother, Murphy McAlister Hickerson, was a homemaker and entrepreneur. Her calling was to make a contribution to humanity through her children. My paternal grandfather, Leroy Alexander, was a chauffeur for the Department of Treasury. My paternal grandmother, Georgia Alexander, was a congressional office housekeeper. Both families had an intentional commitment to Christ expressed through their service in the church and community. They transmitted that to their children, and it took hold in their lives.

My father, Claude Alexander Sr., was the younger of two

children. His older sister, Shirley, pursued a career in psychology, serving in both hospital and private practices. Meanwhile, his interests focused on electronics, which he pursued in the army as a radar technician. After serving in the military, he became a technical writer for several military-related companies.

My mother, Otrie Hickerson, was the only daughter of five children. Her early aspiration was to become a teacher. My grandfather gently nudged her interests toward the medical field, however, particularly toward psychiatry. This was a bold aspiration for a Black woman. In the mid-to-late 1950s, few Black women attended medical schools, and even fewer specialized in psychiatry.

My parents met and courted during my mother's undergrad and medical school years at Howard University in Washington, DC. They married several years later, after my mother completed her medical internship in 1963.

I was born on January 22, 1964, at Schoitz Memorial Hospital in Waterloo, Iowa. (Yes, Iowa does have Black people in it.) My mother was fulfilling her psychiatric residency at the Mental Health Institute in Independence, Iowa. My parents' union ended a year later, though their relationship remained cordial.

Following her residency, my mother and I moved to Topeka, Kansas, where she served as a staff psychiatrist at the prestigious Meninger Foundation until 1967 when the opportunity arose to return to DC. We moved back to her hometown where she served as the chief psychiatrist in the outpatient department at Area B Community Health Center for Washington, DC's Department of Public Health. She also became a clinical instructor in psychiatry at Howard University College of Medicine.

Her primary role, however, was to instill in me a knowledge and love of Jesus. And she did! She often spoke to me about Christ and taught me the Scriptures. From her, I learned to love hymns and understand the significance of prayer. Oft times, after attending church, we returned home and had church again. I recited the Bible verse I learned and imitated the preacher. We then opened the door of the house as a sign of extending an invitation to join. On the first Sunday of each month, we shared communion. Little did she know the seeds she was planting. The first harvest of fruit was when I accepted Christ in the third grade.

Awakening to Racial Sensitivity

On the evening of April 4, 1968, Mama and I were watching television when the network suddenly interrupted the program. Dr. Martin Luther King Jr.'s photo covered the screen with the announcement that he had been assassinated. Immediately, Mama burst into uncontrollable weeping.

I had never seen her weep in such a manner, especially so suddenly and unexpectedly. At the age of four, I couldn't comprehend what was happening or why. Who was the man on the screen who would cause my mother to respond in such a way? Later that evening, she explained to me who he was, what he was doing, and why he was so important. But it was still difficult to fully grasp.

Living on the outer rim of Northwest DC, we stayed somewhat insulated from the explosive reaction that occurred in the District following Dr. King's assassination. What began as a peaceful protest mushroomed into a four-day riot, resulting in thirteen deaths due to the fires, police officer shootings, or the rioters themselves. Nearly 1,100 people were injured and 7,600 arrested.[1]

Prompted by a courtship and engagement to a medical-school classmate and the challenge to become the first Black psychiatrist in Mississippi, as well as the first Black to join the Mississippi Psychiatric Association, Mama moved us to Jackson in the summer of '68.

Her fiancé, Dr. Robert Smith, who became my stepfather in 1969, is the ninth son in a family of ten boys and two girls.

His father, Joe, made his living in livestock and farming. His mother, Wilma, was a homemaker and milliner. They raised their children with a fierce determination for self-sufficiency and Christian faith.

At an early age, Robert was recognized as a prodigy in academics. Being the tenth of the twelve children, his older siblings gave time and attention to his pursuits. In his junior high-school years, he developed an interest in medicine. After graduating from Howard University Medical School and completing his medical residency in Chicago, he returned to Mississippi where he believed he was needed. That sense of call motivated him to establish a private practice in Jackson in 1962.

One year later, upon the assassination of his friend and cohort Medgar Evers, he and Drs. John Holloman and Walter Lear formed the Medical Committee for Civil Rights (MCCR), which petitioned the American Medical Association (AMA) to oppose unequivocally discrimination in health care against the Black patient and physician. Pictures of their picketing the AMA were published by the *New York Times,* bringing international attention to discrimination in America's health care and leading to the desegregation of the AMA. The following year, he and other colleagues formed the Medical Committee for Human Rights (MCHR), which served as the medical corps for the Civil Rights Movement. MCHR provided care for civil rights workers and local people active in the movement who could not obtain appropriate medical care. It became Daddy's role to provide medical care for Dr. John Perkins and medical coverage for Dr. Martin Luther King Jr. and others when they were in Mississippi.

Our move to Jackson and Mama's marriage set an environment of immense investment and challenge. Our household held no delineation between service to God and service to the community. I was continually exposed to such heroes and heroines of the Civil Rights Movement as Charles Evers, Fannie Lou Hamer, Stokely Carmichael, Julian Bond, Andy Young, Drew Days, Margaret Walker Alexander, and others. Those times made a powerful impression on me and gave me context for my own experience of racial brokenness and division in personal and profound ways.

After spending the first grade in an all-Black Christian school, my parents put me in a predominantly White Catholic school, where I was the only Black in my second-grade class. With the public schools going through desegregation, my parents felt that the Catholic school system would be a safer place to land and engage. This was my first experience of being an absolute minority. It wasn't long after the start of school that I was made to know my place as a minority.

One day on the playground, a boy, whom I thought was a friend, called me the "N" word. Everyone began to laugh. While I had not heard that word before, by the way he said it and the reaction of everyone, I knew it wasn't positive. That evening, when I told Mama, I remember the look on her face, the pause in her speech, and the grief in her posture. Hers was the awareness of the loss of my innocence as it related to race. For the first time, her son was made to feel the negative value of his color. Having felt a sense of place in every other learning environment, I now felt out of place. How would she explain to me the meaning of the word, and the reaction of my classmates, in a way that would build me up with the courage to reenter that environment and learn?

While I don't remember everything about her explanation to me that night, I do remember the care in her words and the look on her face. I remember her saying that it was more about them than it was about me. I remember the challenge that I would have to be twice as good to be considered equal.

This knowledge prompted a notion within me that for a Black boy, simply being is not enough to belong. I must be super, extra, exceptional, remarkable. The desire never to feel what I felt pressured me to perform in ways that were undeniably positive, but burdensome all the same. One humorous coping strategy I employed was noticing that my classmates liked the cartoon television series Jonny Quest. Johnny's best friend was Hadji, one of the few characters of color on cartoons. Because none of us distinguished Hadji as being Middle Eastern Indian, I told them that Hadji was my cousin. Their tone changed immediately. I was accepted because of my perceived proximity to one whom they saw as acceptable.

Even as I write this story, I lament how early it was for me to be saddled with such a burden. Yet I am mindful of how that burden of being exceptional to be considered equal continues for people of color.

God Stirrings

I survived that year, and the following year, Mama and Daddy transferred me to a predominantly Black Catholic elementary, which I attended until I transitioned to a racially mixed Catholic middle school. During my eighth-grade year, I began to feel God stirring me toward religious vocation. One of the priests discerned it and gave great support to what was just a tiny mustard seed.

In high school, I encountered an English teacher named William Avalon who saw a shy ninth grader and called him "The Great Alexander." Throughout the next four years, he engaged me in the wonder of literature, the world of thought and ideas, and the grace of genuine love and concern. Where he saw racism and racial brokenness, he demonstrated the courage to address it among his colleagues and students. He exemplified what solidarity with people of color was and was willing to shoulder the weight of that solidarity.

I also found myself reconnected with some of my second-grade classmates. None of us mentioned the experience on the playground or my Hadji relative. They may have forgotten.

Either way, we were cordial. Later on, I received the support of many of those classmates to become the first person of color elected student body vice president.

It was also in high school that God further impressed His call to the ministry of the gospel. I finally yielded at the end of my senior year. To prepare for ministry work, after graduation, I headed to Atlanta and Morehouse College in 1981. My time there began in the wake of serial killer Wayne Williams' arrest in connection to killing two men as well as at least twenty-three children, known as the Atlanta Child Murders.

College was quite a shift in environment from my high school in Jackson. Atlanta was establishing itself as the Mecca for progressive Black thought and activity. The Atlanta University Center, comprised of Atlanta University, Clark College, More-house College, Morris Brown College, Spelman College, and the Interdenominational Center, was at the center of it all. There I was exposed to leaders in various fields who modeled excellence and civic commitment. Morehouse was unabashed in its expecta-tion of its graduates to lead in positively transforming society and uplifting the marginalized and oppressed. My time spent there, learning history coupled with becoming more aware of how men and women were leading in civil rights, produced in me a self-ef-ficacy necessary to endure, confront, transcend, and transform any racial bias and discrimination I faced.

The opportunity to attend seminary and learn from two uncles who pastored in Western Pennsylvania led me to Pitts-burgh Theological Seminary in 1985, where I earned a master of divinity degree in 1988, and which opened the door for me to take my first pastorate at Morning Star Baptist Church in West Mifflin, Pennsylvania.

The church was sandwiched between a public-housing development and a residential neighborhood. My time there came during the aftermath of steel mills closing and corporate headquarters exiting Pittsburgh. I saw firsthand the damage and disintegration of community ecosystems due to corporate decline and dislocation. I became sensitized to the fragility of community fabric and the need for a gospel that meets people at the intersection of despair and hope in meaningful ways. My time in Pittsburgh also introduced me to active engagement through multiracial interdenominational coalitions.

This was my first foray into what I later called cultural translation—the ability to speak a truth, an experience, a perception, or an understanding in ways that a person or people of a different race, ethnicity, or culture can understand and come to appreciate for themselves.

I experienced this first at a multiracial Martin Luther King Jr. holiday community service in Upper St. Clair, Pennsylvania. Upper St. Clair is a bedroom township to Pittsburgh. This took place while many Blacks were still tender from an occurrence in Boston on October 23, 1989. Charles Stuart, a White man, called the police and said that a Black man named Willie Bennett shot him and his pregnant wife, who died seventeen days after successfully delivering her baby by C-section. Without any other interviews or forensic checks, the police immediately began to search a mostly Black area in Boston called Mission Hill. Only after Charles' brother told police that Charles committed the murder did the police begin to look into the inconsistencies of his statement.[2]

His was the latest within a history of Whites committing crimes and falsely accusing Blacks, based on the widespread notion of Black criminality. With that as the backdrop, I realized the importance of speaking about the biblical truth that sets us free, in a way that also responded to the current state of culture. Sharing the Good News was not just a matter of offering biblical exegesis but cultural translation.

This recognition became more fully developed after I moved to Charlotte, North Carolina, in 1990 to pastor the University Park Baptist Church, a seventy-seven-year-old predominantly Black congregation. I spent those early years simply being present among the people, getting into their hearts and allowing them to get into mine. I also found it essential to set a strong biblical foundation through teaching to establish the sheet of music from which we all would sing.

An important event happened my second year of ministry there. I met my wife, Kimberly, on a blind date on October 15, 1992. I was taken by the quickness and depth of her answers to questions I asked. I was struck by her leaving a good post in Washington, DC, to return home and help care for her dad who had multiple sclerosis. That action revealed a substantial capacity for love, and caused me to believe that the man who had the fortune of entering into her heart would be blessed. I relentlessly gave pursuit to becoming that man. We got engaged on December 31 and were married the following year on November 27, 1993.

Engaging with the Community

As the congregation solidified and grew, the attention of the community increased. This came partly as a result of being seen as responsive to community issues and needs. One of the most problematic issues in Charlotte has been education, particularly student assignment. In the 1990s Charlotte was still under a judicial order that mandated busing as a means of school desegregation and achieving quality of education—the burden of which was disproportionately placed upon students of color waking up early and traveling the farthest distances.

As more people moved to Charlotte, the suburbs mushroomed, leading to a demand for new schools. As they were built, the schools in the inner city lacked substantial investment. This created a tension between parents living in the outer north and south desiring student assignments at the new schools in their neighborhoods. Opposition to their students being bused anywhere became intense. A new school superintendent introduced a vision for magnet schools. The system would invest money in updating certain inner-city schools and delivering cutting-edge programs to attract suburban, mainly White students to travel into the city and attend these schools. While noble in intent, the unconscious messaging couldn't have been worse. The message was that upgrading and updating schools within Black communities could be done only out of a desire to attract White students from the suburbs.

This situation became my entrance into the community as a cultural translator. My response was first to understand the various dynamics at play by providing a space within our church for people to voice their concerns. My second response was to be part of a broader multiracial cadre of individuals to give voice of critique and call for an inclusive process that took into account the diversity of the Charlotte-Mecklenburg community. Though the school board ultimately voted to approve the superintendent's plan, I felt that we had succeeded in giving them much to consider as it related to implementing that plan.

I continued to engage in causes related to education, which eventually led to my joining the board of the Charlotte-Mecklenburg Urban League in 1994, where I served for nine years, including the last four as its chair.

During this period, with the help of the Industrial Areas Foundation, an interdenominational and multiracial group of churches came together to form HELP (Helping Empower Local People). Our aim was to identify the stubborn and sticky matters of our city, particularly in the areas of education and economic development, and to work with institutions in developing common-sense solutions. The strategies varied depending upon the issue and the institution. Sometimes our work involved direct action and confrontation. Other times we engaged through subtle diplomacy and partnering. What I learned in that process is that there are no permanent allies or enemies; it is permanent interest.

Between 1993 and 1996, White police officers used violence that resulted in three questionable deaths of unarmed Black citizens. By the third occurrence, Charlotte was on the verge of social unrest. To their credit, Charlotte's mayor and the chair of the County Commission asked the CEO of the Foundation for the Carolinas to sponsor a community-engagement process, called the Community Building Task Force, that diverse individuals would lead. The charge was to hold a variety of public forums to prepare the community for a two-day summit to address the matter of race.

I accepted the invitation to be part of what was supposed to be a six-month commitment. We identified education, public safety, economic development, and housing as subjects of interest. We developed issue-action groups around each, co-led by an institutional stakeholder and a community leader. These issue-action groups held forums that engaged the community around a particular subject, viewing it through the lens of race, and developed specific strategies to address concerns that were raised.

The two-day summit was then held in December 1997. In the debrief, one conclusion became clear: the work had only just begun. The Community Building Task Force became the Community Building Initiative (CBI), with a mission of "giving people and organizations the knowledge, skills, and courage to fight bias, remove barriers to opportunity, and build a more equitable and just Charlotte-Mecklenburg."[3] I had the pleasure to serve as a co-chair from 1999 to 2012.

My involvement with CBI paralleled serving in other institutions, such as the Charlotte Arts and Science Council, the United

Way of Central Carolinas, Charlotte Chamber of Commerce, the Civil Service board, and the Human Services board.

One of the more disappointing and difficult tasks during this period was getting evangelicals engaged in the conversation around race. Many viewed it as unnecessary and peripheral to the gospel. So we struggled to get support for many goals we were pursuing. Fortunately, not all evangelicals felt that way, and we were able to garner enough support within the center and mid-ring of the city to incent change within many organizations that were affecting the public.

As I served the community and church, I was delighted to watch God work in our midst, particularly in the life of our church. The late 1990s and early 2000s saw explosive growth for our congregation, leading us to acquire property where we could build a sanctuary, education wing, and family life and wellness center. Then we acquired two other properties in South and East Charlotte to serve as congregational meeting sites.

The Blessed Power of Relationships

So much of my life has been blessed by God's gift of favored relationships where people see something in me that I don't see in myself and provide the space for what they sense or see to manifest. The first to recognize God's call on my life were my maternal uncles, Reverends Carl (deceased), Willis, Charles (deceased), and Ernest Hickerson, who, after discerning the sincerity of that call, provided every opportunity for me to grow in the gifts of preaching and teaching. They modeled a pastoral heart and care for people. My uncle Charles developed a love of preaching and an appreciation for the words in the Word of God. My uncle Willis has been a counselor, pastor, and cheerleader, and serves as our church's minister to pacesetters (seniors).

The second is Bishop Walter Thomas, pastor of New

Psalmist Baptist Church in Baltimore, Maryland. While he served as president of the Hampton University Ministers Conference, he provided me the platform opportunity to serve as the morning preacher for the conference, the oldest and largest interdenominational gathering of African-American clergy in the country. This set the stage for me to later enter the pipeline of leadership, which eventually led to my serving as president from 2011 to 2014. He continues to cover me as a pastor, mentor me as a son, and challenge me as a leader.

A third is Leighton Ford, whose mentoring and care opened the door for me to join the Gordon-Conwell Theological Seminary board and to attend the 2010 third Lausanne International Congress on World Evangelization in Cape Town, South Africa. I had no idea how much my life would change as a result. Even more than that, Leighton and his wife, Jean, have opened their hearts and their lives to Kim and me.

In October 2010, I joined more than three thousand people from around the world in Cape Town for Lausanne, a conference believed to be the most diverse gathering of Christians in the church's modern era. It was the first time I was caught by the breadth of the church. Two-thirds of the participants were from the global East and South. I saw an evangelicalism that was devoid of the cultural captivity of politics. And it was there that I understood a word that God had spoken in my spirit nine years prior.

In 2001, I was seriously considering a run for mayor of Charlotte. I had backing from the community and corporate sectors. I asked the church to commit to a time of prayer over it. God responded to that prayer during a service at the Hampton University Ministers Conference. He spoke four words: *Charlotte is too small.* I didn't understand that message at the time. As I sat in the sessions at Cape Town, however, I came to grasp God's heart and purpose for me being tied to His purpose for the world.

In Cape Town I also had another providential moment in which I met Doug Birdsall, who was leading the Lausanne Movement at the time, and Harold Smith, CEO of Christianity Today International, a publishing organization. Those introductions led to personal relationships as well as opportunities of further service with Lausanne and Christianity Today.

For instance, Doug Birdsall invited me to speak at the 2013 Lausanne Global Leaders' Summit in Bangalore, India. While there, I met a man who would quickly become my friend, Mac Pier. God used our time together in Bangalore for Mac to share the vision for city movements that engages the whole of the church to address the hard facts of the city in ways that catalyze collaboration and create greater readiness and acceptance of the gospel. I didn't need much urging to join that vision. And for the past eight years, I have served with Mac as a board member of Movement.org.

Cape Town 2010 set the stage for my serving in places I never sought nor imagined, such as Wycliffe Bible Translators USA, BioLogos, Council for Christian Colleges and Universities, and InterVarsity Christian Fellowship. It has been in the course of those places that I have also provided cultural translation. Many of these organizations had their beginnings in eras of racial segregation and division. As such, being primarily White for many years, they found themselves needing and seeking to embrace the increasing diversity that is both the United States and the world of the church. I have been blessed to see the openness and courage among those institutions to embrace the moment.

God's words to me were correct. Through my work within the community and the church, I've learned that His heart beats for the church as a whole to come together and seek conciliation and unity. I want to be part of that team. I want that for you too.

Chapter 2

ORIGINS IN BLACK AND WHITE: MAC'S STORY

A nswering God's call to overcome racial division has required a conscious decision for me. The journey toward this decision began with the intersection of my parents' lives during the Korean War. My father's family were bankers from South Dakota. My mother's family were farmers from South Carolina.

My mother, Helen McKenzie, was one of thirteen children, two having died at a young age. She grew up during the Great Depression, having been born in 1932 in Kingstree, South Caroline. Her father, Harmon McKenzie, died when she was eleven, leaving her mother, Arcie, to raise her and her siblings largely as a single mom. To survive, my mother and her siblings worked in the fields by hand under the scorching South Carolinian sun to raise their crops. During that time, my mother was also able to attend nursing school after she graduated high school. I have yet to meet anyone with my mother's work ethic. She molded that ethic into my siblings and me, which has served us well in our lives and career choices.

My father, Richard Pier, was also born at the beginning of the Great Depression in 1931 in Yankton, South Dakota. Because his family were bankers, they, alongside their community, felt the brunt of the financial crisis. As with so many others who lived during that time, my grandmother Mae Pier became frugal with everything, including saving and reusing aluminum foil. My father was fortunate that his grandfather Tom Pier had started the local bank in 1914. It was the eighteenth chartered bank in the state of South Dakota. His son, Ralph Pier, my grandfather, worked in the bank until he died unexpectedly at the age of forty-seven. My father became a third-generation bank president, followed by my brother, Rick, who became the fourth-generation bank president.

Before his fourth year at the University of South Dakota Business School, my father enlisted in the air force during the Korean War. Dad was assigned to be a musician in the air force marching band. He also played piano in a jazz band.

He was stationed at Shaw Air Force Base in Sumter, South Carolina, where he met my mother at an officer party in the summer of 1954. They married in June 1955. And the following year, in 1956, my mother gave birth to my sister Renee.

Upon completion of his military career, my father relocated my mom and Renee back to South Dakota where he was set to finish his final year of schooling. During his senior year, his father, Ralph, died suddenly from a heart condition. Before he could finish school, Dad was plunged into the family business. As his professional career grew, so did his family. They added my brother Rick in 1957, my twin sister, Michele, and me in 1958, and our sister Erin in 1962.

For all intents and purposes, our family life was uneventful. And our community, though just a few miles away from an Indian reservation, was largely homogeneous. Of everyone in our nuclear family, my mother had the most interaction with people of other races, since she had been born and raised in the South.

My only real interaction with people who looked different

from me was when we would visit my maternal grandmother in South Carolina. But even then, they were surface interactions at best, perhaps seeing African Americans in a grocery store or at a gas station. For most of my life, I was unaware of the troubled racial histories of both of my parents' home states. And since I carried that ignorance, racial issues didn't seem all that pressing. They didn't affect me, so I was uninterested.

A Little History Lesson

What I didn't understand growing up was that history isn't just in the past. It directly affects the present and future—who we are and who we become. The old saying goes, "Those who don't know history are doomed to repeat it." We are all shaped by historical forces that are out of our control. Forces of history that I didn't know about . . .

Both South Dakota and South Carolina have troubled racial histories. South Dakota is home to several Sioux tribes, which make up the Sioux Nation,[1] who were in significant conflict with the US government in the nineteenth century. Following the 1803 Louisiana Purchase, initiated by President Thomas Jefferson, as well as the development of the transcontinental railroad, the United States expanded rapidly with European immigration. Western-traveling immigrants looking for a better life ran smack into Native American tribes from Georgia to Oklahoma to South Dakota. Bloody conflict ensued that resulted in a stain on the American conscience on both sides of the conflict. Entire families were scalped on both sides.

The American Indian conflicts were bloody affairs that ultimately saw a conquered people relegated to reservations. A migrant way of life across thousands of miles of prairies was gone, for indigenous peoples were gone. There are now nine reservations across South Dakota. I grew up sixteen miles from Yankton tribal lands.

South Carolina was the first Southern state to secede from the Union in 1860. At the time of the Civil War, more enslaved people than free were living in the state.[2] My mother grew up in Williamsburg County. As of 2018, the percentage of African Americans was 64.4 percent in Williamsburg County, as opposed to 31.2 percent Caucasian.[3]

As an every-other-year visitor to my grandmother's home in South Carolina, I saw the cultural divide in the community. I was struck by the number of African Americans there and the limited number of interactions across cultural lines. Everyone was separate, and nobody seemed all that bothered about it. In fact, some people wanted it that way.

When I was ten years old, my family and I were visiting some friends in Myrtle Beach, a popular vacation destination in South Carolina. The subject of race came up with one of the friends, and I explained that we did not have any African Americans in our community in South Dakota.

"That sounds like heaven to me," she said.

Her words jarred me. Even though I had very little spiritual understanding at the time, the idea that heaven was described as a place where an entire ethnic group was absent seemed wrong. But it began to create suspicion in me toward African Americans.

Years later after moving to New York City, I met an African-American pastor living in Paterson, New Jersey. We both attended Concerts of Prayer Greater New York's annual Pastor's Prayer Summit. I asked the pastor where his family was from.

"South Carolina."

"Where in South Carolina?"

"Kingstree."

Kingstree is my mother's hometown, so I asked, "What's your name?"

"Moses McKenzie," he said.

McKenzie is my mother's last name. I could not help but wonder if someone in my past had owned someone in his past.

While working in the family bank during my high-school summers, I had occasional interactions with Native Americans. Our town of Avon had a popular furniture store, Powers Furniture, that was a favorite place to shop for several area Native Americans. Oftentimes the Native Americans would buy furniture from the store with borrowed money from our family bank. If a Native American decided not to repay the loan, the bank had no recourse, given the political sovereignty of Indian reservations. The fruit of that experience was a growing mistrust of people who were different from me. By the time I entered my high-school years, I had developed a dual prejudice against Native Americans and African Americans. This prejudice was rooted in a fundamental suspicion of the other. If persons were different, I concluded, they could not be trusted.

The Great Disequilibrium

My family were faithful attenders of the local Presbyterian church. And even though I attended Sunday school, went through church confirmation, and was a regular at my church's youth group, I didn't give much thought to how my faith might intersect with my prejudices—or my daily life, for that matter.

But something was changing within me. In 1976, when I was seventeen years old, I was involved in a near death car accident that shook me to the core. I began reading my Bible more frequently and feeling a spiritual hunger to learn more about God. That summer, I had been invited to take a Bible camp staffing assignment in North Dakota for the camp's newspaper. As I participated in the camp, that spiritual hunger grew. And on July 20, 1976, in the back of the cafeteria, I invited Jesus to take control of my life.

Not only did my life change, so did my mindset and attitudes. For the first time in my life, I encountered an awakening to inclusion. I experienced my conversion in two parts: a conversion to the Person of Jesus and a conversion to the people of Jesus. I knew instinctively that followers of Jesus belonged to him and to one another. And we needed others to know about that kind of inclusive love that Jesus offered.

Within three weeks of my conversion to Jesus, I had brought all the local youth groups together to do a film outreach in our small town. Two months after my conversion, as I began my senior year, I started and led a before-school Bible study. It gained so much attention that 20 percent of the student body became involved. We were seeing a mini spiritual awakening on our high-school campus.

My spiritual fervor continued into my college years. While attending the University of South Dakota, my father's alma mater, I worked with my InterVarsity group and the Campus Crusade group to lead campus-wide outreaches. My college roommate, Mark Theissen, the Campus Crusade student president, and I spoke about the gospel in nine of the fourteen fraternities and sororities on campus.

During my freshman year, I also took on another interest. Her name was Marya. She came from an evangelical Lutheran background with very godly parents and grandparents. Her grandfather was a lay pastor who walked for miles in the winter to open the church on Sunday morning to heat the building. Marya's sister, Janet, was a missionary to China and became a lay pastor of their home church in rural Langford, South Dakota. In addition to being very attractive, it was Marya's spiritual passion that drew me to her, something we both continued to cultivate in our lives through our involvement with InterVarsity.

In my junior year, we had twenty students from our InterVarsity group attend the Urbana '79 Missions Conference, where Billy Graham challenged us to go anywhere in the world that God would send us. Marya and I responded to that call.

That Urbana commitment led to me join the InterVarsity staff in 1981, after my graduation. I oversaw six campuses for the next three years in eastern South Dakota. In December 1982, my now-bride, Marya, and I served as staff at an International House Party with students from across the globe. In 1983, we took our first overseas mission trip to Bihar, North India. In a state the size of Nebraska, we lived among one hundred million people. The ratio of Hindus and Muslims to Christians was one hundred thousand to one. For ten weeks we were plunged into an environment in which we were a persecuted minority. We prayed three to nine hours every Friday as a community. The premier lesson from that summer was that only corporate prayer can overcome the greatest challenges we face—whether they be spiritual, relational, or racial.

Seeing poverty and spiritual darkness on that scale rocked our worlds. We saw people surviving on a few dollars a month. One tribal group in Bihar was made up of 75 million people without a single verse of Scripture in their language. We also saw the power of community, as our team of Muslim converts, Hindu converts, and diverse Indian community worked together to share the gospel in that context—wildly diverse communities powerfully transformed by Jesus and expressing the gospel to anyone who would listen.

When Marya and I returned home, we struggled with our newfound understanding and trying to slip back into the homogenous and "normal" life of South Dakota. But we could not. We knew we would never be the same. And that meant we had to do something different with our lives.

A Third Conversion

In June 1984, Marya and I sold our possessions and moved to New York City with InterVarsity. In an act of obedience, we were heading there with the plan to return to India within two years. This was a high-risk adventure for us: Marya was three months pregnant, we had no permanent place to live, and we had insufficient financial support.

What we did have was Marya's younger brother, Mark, who had moved to New York City two years before for an InterVarsity summer internship program and had stayed. Mark was placed with a Caribbean church, Bethel Gospel Tabernacle, in Jamaica, Queens. He had been embraced by the Caesar family who led the church. Mark lived with the Caesar family for a season.

Remarkably and generously, the Caesar family took us in and offered us thirty days rent-free to figure out our housing. This African-American family with Caribbean roots had met my normal instincts of mistrust across racial lines with hospitality. It was so unexpected! Their kindness and hospitality taught us that the most powerful thing this side of heaven is being radically loved by someone radically different. It completely blew apart all my mistrust and incorrect suspicions toward those of a different race. And it was so powerful because they did it with such generous intention. I could no longer hold onto those wayward beliefs when faced with such Christlikeness.

This was the third conversion. The Caesars showed us by example what it means to have a relentless, pursuing commitment to unity. This commitment needed to be expressed in the most practical of ways. Our need was housing. They met that need. Our skin color made absolutely no difference to them or to the way they treated us.

The Caesar family has been the one familial thread in our

lives to New York City since 1984. Even today we continue to work on joint mission efforts together.

In our first six years in New York City from 1984 to 1990, we were plunged into the world of multiethnicity, both in the city and in the church. We began to attend First Baptist Church in Flushing, which had members speaking sixty languages. Our work with InterVarsity engaged leaders from African-American, Caribbean, Hispanic, Chinese, Korean, and Anglo backgrounds. We were stunned to see the respect and receptivity we received from those so different from ourselves. And again, it brought me a profound sense of gratitude as I considered how wrong all those misconceptions I'd held onto had been.

My third conversion deepened while I spent a year studying at Trinity Evangelical Divinity School in the 1990–1991 year. I had lived in New York City for six years and needed to write my thesis paper to finish my MA degree. I knew the time was right to study more and write about what I had been learning. The result was *The Response of the White Church to the Black Community,* in which I looked more closely at the formational understanding of the disparities that existed between us. After surveying five hundred primarily White Christians, the only contribution most of them could identify from the African-American community were sports and music.

My research concluded that the two primary experiences of African Americans historically were dehumanization and disadvantage. Claude calls this the "denial of personhood." I resolved that I would do whatever I could to use my agency as a White evangelical to build alliances that resulted in greater opportunity for those who were disadvantaged. It was equally important for White Christians to learn from the extraordinary minority community who have led so powerfully in Metro New York City. I wanted others to discover the truth about race that I was learning.

My engagement was not just academic, it was also deeply spiritual and emotional. One Friday I found myself just sitting in the parking lot of a grocery store. I had just finished reading Alex Haley's *Roots,* describing the experience of his ancestor Kunta Kinte, who had been captured in Africa and enslaved in America. The book told Kunta's and his descendants' experiences all the way up to the author's. It was the most powerful literary experience I had ever had. What made it more powerful was that during that time, the other seminary students and I had been fasting and praying on campus.

While I sat in my car in that parking lot, I began to weep uncontrollably. I had just begun to apprehend what that level of suffering was like. I thought about generations of families who had been torn apart at the slave auction. And one of the great themes of world history—the suffering of people of African descent—began to envelop my mind and heart.

The Context of New York City's Racial Unrest

Our epiphany about Christian faith and unity was not happening in an historical vacuum. When we moved to New York City in 1984, the city was roiling. In December of that year, a German named Bernhard Goetz shot four unarmed African Americans on the subway, believing they were trying to mug him.[4] That action became the fuse that lit the fire of a decadal murder epidemic that rocked New York City.

In 1990 there were eight murders a day for a year.[5] There was so much death that New York City's morgue simply ran out of room.[6] Much of the violence was race related—Arabs killing Jews, Whites killing African Americans, African Americans killing African Americans, and Latino gangs executing bystanders as part of gang initiation.[7]

In the late 1980s, even our Flushing, Queens, neighborhood

was not immune. A Chinese couple was showing the apartment they had purchased as a wedding gift for their son when a robber approached them and killed the mother. Ten days later the man who fit the description of the murderer walked past Marya as she came home from working the night shift as a nurse at a local hospital. The violence of the city had arrived at our backyard.

We knew we needed to do something. So we invited sixteen churches to gather at our home church, First Baptist, in Flushing, Queens, to pray on February 5, 1988. That day seventy-five churches participated. By 1989 the concerts of prayer model that we introduced spread to seven locations. Over the next thirty years we saw two thousand churches participate, representing two hundred and fifty thousand people.

The beauty and the power of these gatherings were that they represented the cultural mosaic of New York City. Our Flushing community speaks one hundred languages. First Baptist attendees spoke sixty languages at one point. As churches gathered across racial and denominational lines, we began experiencing a front-row seat to the vision of John in Revelation 5 where people from "every tribe, language, and tongue" gathered to pray and worship the Lamb.

This praying represented a powerful response to the racial violence of the city. By the late 1990s, we began to see New York City transformed. The murder rate had declined from 2,400 in 1993 to 289 in 2018.

More Than Prayer

The exploding prayer movement provided an opportunity for leaders to encounter one another genuinely and powerfully. It also provided a basis for trusted relationships to grow into important mission expressions. Leaders built alliances and began planting churches together, addressing issues of poverty and relief together, and assisting widows and orphans globally. One of the alliances incubated was the Church Multiplication Alliance.

Dr. Tim Keller began Redeemer Presbyterian Church in 1989—a congregation primarily attended by White and Asian Christians in Manhattan. As the church began to grow and multiply, it took on the expression of diverse churches in New York City.

In 2000 Tim invited me to co-create with him the Church Multiplication Alliance to start new churches in New York City. Our dream was to see 10 percent of Manhattan become evangelical Christian in our lifetimes, up from 1 percent in the 1980s when we both arrived. The alliance attracted theologically diverse churches, from Southern Baptist and Pentecostal to Lutheran and Reformed denominations.

From 1989 to 2009, the alliance's impact saw 300 percent growth of evangelical churches in Manhattan. This represented thirty thousand people in church in 2009 who were not in church in 1989. This research fueled the formation of Movement Day in 2010.

I, along with a small team from Redeemer City to City, birthed Movement Day out of a desire to see the church, united in all its expressions in a city, cause measurable impact on the city because of the gospel. That impact would include new churches being planted, Christianity experiencing numerical growth, as well as social well-being initiatives being incubated (e.g., churches adopting schools, increasing literacy).

At our first Movement Day event in 2010, we had eight hundred leaders from thirty-four states and fourteen countries. Our model was scratching a global itch. Leaders were longing to see the body of Christ in all its diversity and beauty come together to demonstrate the reality of Jesus in a city. How far I had come from the prejudicial days of my South Dakota youth.

Lausanne and Movement Day

Claude referenced the importance of Lausanne in the previous chapter. I was also privileged to attend this historic gathering. The Cape Town Lausanne event happened three weeks after our first Movement Day in 2010. At Cape Town, Tim Keller and I both met with Bob Doll, a globally strategic marketplace leader. He was the chief equity strategist for Black Rock, managing one of the largest investment funds in the world. Doll would join our Movement Day model as a marketplace Christian to influence other marketplace Christians globally. He immediately saw the power and impact of Movement Day to achieve the kind of unity and exponential growth we all longed to see.

By the 2013 Lausanne meeting in Bangalore, I had been asked to serve as the catalyst for cities with Lausanne. While there, I sat in on a session Claude was leading. As I listened to him give exposition of the Scriptures, I was struck by his theological depth and cultural agility. I wanted to meet him.

As we talked that day, I resonated deeply with his vision, values, and passions. And he with mine. I mentioned my desire to acquaint the larger White church with the impact of African-American church leaders. Claude expressed his desire to stay connected to see where the journey would take us. A Black leader and a White leader who met in South India and who began a friendship with a common desire for the church to come to its full beauty globally. What an amazing journey I am privileged to be on.

As I reflect on the past sixty years of my life, I have seen God raise up remarkable mentors and heroes for me from the African-American community. The Caesars showed great hospitality by taking us into their home as an unproven young couple. My ethnically diverse New York City pastoral colleagues showed great humility in allowing me to lead a multiracial prayer movement. And Claude is being used by God to help me see the relentless, transforming nature of God's requirements on my life as a White Christian leader. And I am so incredibly grateful.

Chapter 3

AN INVITATION TO A RACIAL CONVERSATION

Every person has a racial story.

Have you ever taken time to reflect on your unique racial story and how God is using that story to involve you with His Great Story—in which He is reconciling the world to Himself and to one another?

That is what we hope will motivate you as you work through the pages of this book and pursue reconciliation throughout your life and your relationships.

Though our racial stories have always been part of who we are and how we relate to others, the scale of unrest, division, and hardship in the world today makes the conversation on race an urgent and significant one. The church of Jesus Christ is required to work at a level of unity as never experienced before to make a redemptive difference in the world.

In addition, young people today are leaving the church in unprecedented numbers. Part of that reason is because they feel Christianity doesn't hold any relatable significance or value for them. Young people are looking for a transcendent cause that gives meaning to their lives. Only the overwhelming gospel of

Jesus Christ can do that—not only to save sins and cleanse us, but to give us purpose and meaning. Being on the front lines of the issues of redemption in the pain of our cities can attract young people otherwise indifferent to the church today.

To address the needs of our cities, we need a unified witness. Charlotte, North Carolina, where I (Claude) come from, is ranked fiftieth out of fifty in major US cities regarding the migration out of poverty into the middle class according to a Harvard study.[1] This requires an enormous amount of intention on the part of leaders from all racial backgrounds. And not just political leaders or community activists. God is calling church leaders and Christian influencers—*us*—to speak into these situations. We have tremendous opportunity to lend a hand to those who need it, as Jesus Himself said He came to do (see Isaiah 61:1–3). And as His followers, He expects the same of us.

Fighting Against the Stereotypes to Seek Unity

On the eve of the 2016 election, Claude and I (Mac) met by phone with A. R. Bernard from the Christian Cultural Center. Dr. Bernard has grown the largest church on the East Coast and has had a tremendous witness at the highest levels of influence in cities all across the United States.

At that time, many presumed that Hillary Clinton would win the election. The question we discussed during our meeting: "What is at stake for the unity of the White evangelical church and the African-American church in relationship to a Clinton presidency or a Trump presidency?" The concern was that we feared the outcome of the election—regardless of the winner—would further splinter attempts at unifying the church.

While Hillary Clinton won the popular vote by 3 million people, Donald Trump carried more than 80 percent of the counties in America geographically, making him the winner. It was evidence of a deep divide geographically and culturally. After the election, Claude and I appeared together on a Christian television program, in which the host asked how we interpreted the results. While so many leaders—including faith leaders—had used the outcome to further bring politics into their congregational conversations, Claude and I wanted to create a more thoughtful conversation. One in which we looked at the dynamics of race, faith, and politics—but making sure that we kept a careful balance.

The truth is that stereotyping others becomes the enemy of conversation. Every solution must begin with a conversation. And as politics has become more divisive, with character bashing and name calling, we shut down conversations before we even get them started. We must wrestle with *nuance.* As Christ followers we are called to be different—to work hard to *start* and *maintain* conversations and to work *together* toward solutions. Our conversations must be civil, empathetic, and pragmatic. We may not agree on every point, but we must be able to thoughtfully and respectfully state the positions of those with whom we disagree. This creates empathy even in the midst of disagreement.

Living Out Those Conversations and Unity

Mac and I have now been friends for nearly a decade. We truly respect and love each other. We are grateful that our racial makeup and history help to give each of us a fuller picture, not only of each other but also of God's kingdom at work. One of the great things that draws me to our friendship and to this work to which we have been called is that it represents great intention. We have been purposeful in learning from each other and contributing to each other's efforts. To see the kind of change we want to see in our churches, communities, and culture, we both understand that it requires a generosity of spirit on all sides of the conversation. Mac allows me to voice my thoughts and insight, based on my experience as an African American, and I do the same for him.

We have both considered it a great privilege to journey with each other. One of our core convictions is that people can only love that which they know. This is why having intellectual rigor in our conversations is so very important.

When we were six months into our friendship, in 2014, I joined the second annual Movement Day gathering in Dallas at the Kay Bailey Hutchinson Convention Center, where 2,100 people attended. The gathering was described as having the largest number of influential leaders from the Dallas faith community at one time in recent history. Mac and his team brought together Christian leaders from diverse churches, marketplace leaders, next-generation leaders, and nonprofit leaders. At the event, we could all feel such a great sense of celebration in all that the church in Dallas was doing and could do together. I rejoiced with them, and yearned—as I know Mac did—for this same type of unity to take place in every city in the United States and around the globe. It was evident that this movement was committed to being open handed to all persons of diverse backgrounds.

As our friendship deepened, Mac made regular trips to Charlotte to help me and Charlotte colleagues birth Movement Day Charlotte in 2018 under the leadership of Rob Kelly and his team from For Charlotte. In our first two years, more than two thousand leaders gathered in Charlotte to consider ways to impact our city practically.

Then in September 2019, when I hosted the R400 Conference at my church in Charlotte, to remember the impact of African slavery over four hundred years and to look at current realities and the future possibilities for people of African descent, Mac was right there in attendance, seeking to gain a deeper and broader perspective on the extraordinary leaders God has raised up in the African-American, African, and African-diaspora communities. This is what being the church is all about—caring about and for one another and our distinct histories and experiences.

So What Is Required of Us to Make This a Reality?

In Micah 6:8, the prophet writes, "He has shown you, O mortal, what is good. And what does the LORD require of you? To act justly and to love mercy and to walk humbly with your God." God is requiring of us a commitment to justice, mercy, and humility.

In August 2020, near the anniversary of Martin Luther King Jr.'s March on Washington, DC, in 1963, I (Claude) noticed signs that held the same messages as they did in 1963. King spoke about bringing a check before the bank of democracy and it always coming back as having insufficient funds. What causes us to keep presenting a check that keeps bouncing? The reason is because God's command is still there. God's requirement has not changed. We continue because we trust God's requirement. I know and believe that God's requirement is going to be fulfilled sooner or later.

For me (Mac), Micah 6:8 has been a family verse that Marya and I chose after we were married in 1980. This verse informed our major life decisions to move to New York City, to spend time in India, to be involved philanthropically with the cause of widows and orphans. When we began to sponsor our first child from Ethiopia in 1982, just before the Ethiopian famine took the lives of one million Ethiopians from starvation, we became deeply moved by the suffering and the resilience of friends and family of African descent. Part of our journey has been the thrill of seeing friends and churches we worked with to sponsor eleven thousand children of African and Haitian descent impacting six hundred thousand persons through the strategy of World Vision. In our immediate family our children have married spouses from Brazilian, Filipino, and Indian backgrounds. Our children and their families speak six languages.

Textually, the three words attached to the word *require*—to do justice, walk humbly, and love mercy—are in the infinitive position. That means that these requirements from God toward each of us as His followers *never end*. It has been a forty-year journey with this verse and the demands of it are as important and necessary today as they ever have been.

Face it, at some point in his or her vocation, every pastor has preached on this passage. We have memorized it. We have heard the passage taught in many contexts. The danger is that the verse is so familiar, it can become unfamiliar. But let's slow down for a while and really spend time thinking about these three words and what they mean.

Let's start with humility. Humility is recognizing who I am before God. That causes me to then present myself no less than I am and no more than I am. It is this constant awareness that, before God, I am limited, imperfect, and needy. The ability to recognize this reality in myself should move me to recognize that in others as well, and therefore, I can treat them by giving them grace, the way in which I receive grace. Walking humbly before God or with God is about trusting Him—both in terms of the action that we are to take and the outcome. Ultimately, humility is the ability to trust God's direction for us and then to act upon that faith and trust in long-term ways that honor and please Him.

In addition, we can think about humility horizontally. I think of the first hymn of the early church from Philippians 2, which draws the relationship between humility and humiliation:

Do nothing out of selfish ambition or vain conceit. Rather, in humility value others above yourselves, not looking to your own interests but each of you to the interests of the others.

In your relationships with one another, have the same mindset as Christ Jesus:

Who, being in very nature God, did not consider equality with God something to be used to his own advantage; rather, he made himself nothing by taking the very nature of a servant, being made in human likeness. And being found in appearance as a man, he humbled himself by becoming obedient to death—even death on a cross!

Therefore God exalted him to the highest place and gave him the name that is above every name, that at the name of Jesus every knee should bow, in heaven and on earth and under the earth, and every tongue acknowledge that Jesus Christ is Lord, to the glory of God the Father. (Philippians 2:3–11)

In humility we become surrendered, almost enslaved, to the needs of others. That is the posture Jesus took toward us. He was humiliated by His death on the cross. He was enslaved to our spiritual and relational need to be reconciled to God and to others.

This is the posture God invites us into. We demonstrate humility when we become enslaved to the needs of others. We see the *imago Dei*—the image of God—in the other person, especially when the other person is different. There could be no greater difference in the universe than when we are compared to who God is.

On the topic of mercy: mercy is a loyal covenant love and faithfulness. It also gives this notion of feeling what the other is feeling. It is being able to get into the skin of another person and being able to see what they see, hear what they hear, and feel what they feel.

Those two things together—the faithfulness in relationship and this ability to feel—in mercy, those things come together. In Lamentations, when Jeremiah says, "It is of the LORD's mercy that we are not consumed, because his compassions fail not. . . . Great is thy faithfulness" (3:22–23), these three things are tied together. It is the Lord's mercy. It is His faithful love, His covenant loyalty, and His compassion. The Hebrew word *racham* refers to mercy, compassion, womb, and bowels. It speaks to the intensity and depth of feeling similar to that of a mother carrying a child in her womb or that of something in your gut that cannot be ignored. These are the things to which God calls us, wrapped up in that term *loving mercy*.

Mercy is proactive kindness. It is not just sentimental, it is intentional. We have to stress the difference between sentiment and intention. We can feel sorry for people (sentiment). But mercy does something about it (intention). The book of Ruth is centered on this theme of kindness. Ruth was merciful toward her mother-in-law, Naomi, as demonstrated in leaving her family to journey back to Bethlehem. She worked in the fields by hand to provide for them. Finally, she followed Naomi's direction to find a mate in Boaz, which resulted in a son as part of the messianic lineage. God always uses mercy as a way to unveil his redemptive character.

Then as we consider justice, we look at what each person has the right to expect under the law. What is due each person under the law, and the equal experience of that expectation. There are two aspects of justice. One is establishing what is right. The other is the notion of vindication. When we look at the foundation of the United States, the nation began with the establishment of what was right—that all people are created equal and are endowed by God with certain inalienable rights. But in practice, that did not flow to everyone. We in the United States have been in this constant pursuit of vindication.

While some nations are just beginning to establish what is right, this desire for justice has gone unmet for centuries in others. America is relatively young. Our discussion is particular, but it is not unique.

Justice is about making right what is wrong, what is unfair. It is correcting an imbalance.

We can find justice throughout the Old Testament, beginning with the Law and continuing through Psalms, Proverbs, and the Prophets. God had standards of conduct for His people that would be just and that would mirror His conduct. That call to justice is particularly strong in Isaiah with six references. It is included in the great messianic prophesy of Isaiah 9: "Of the greatness of his government and peace there will be no end. He will reign on David's throne and over his kingdom, establishing and upholding it with justice and righteousness from that time on and forever. The zeal of the LORD Almighty will accomplish this" (v. 7). The New Testament presumes and builds upon the Old Testament's posture, demands, and expectations.

If you are looking for the words *social justice* throughout these pages, please know that when we speak of justice, it includes the societal aspects. Study of the Scriptures reveals that God's standard of justice needed no qualifying adjective, because it was understood to be both individual and institutional.

It is time for us to step up and do that which God requires of us.

To that end, we offer this book. As you read, we hope you will feel empowered to pursue that call. We hope that you will have an epiphany regarding the character of God and the commands of God on your life and on the lives God puts in your path to influence.

As you work your way through this book, we present a challenge to you—a two-part assignment, if you will. The first part is to focus on your own personal transformation. Be open to learning things about yourself that you did not previously know. Claude and I have learned a great deal about each other and ourselves as we have worked together on this book. What you learn will give you more context to the discussion on justice, humility, and mercy.

The second part of your assignment has to do with how you interact in your city. We are dual citizens: we have citizenship in the kingdom of God, and we are also citizens of the cities where God has planted us. Focus on what is happening in your city and how you can use your agency to make a difference.

Many conversations regarding race, especially recently, have not been a matter of what; they have become a matter of how. Our prayer is that this book can provide one of the answers to the how.

Chapter 4

THE CONSISTENT
REQUIREMENT

On Wednesday, August 28, 1963, more than 250,000 people gathered at the Mall in Washington, DC, for the cause of jobs and freedom. Set before the eyes of the world, multiple generations of Blacks and Whites gave voice and vision for the civil and economic rights of African Americans. On that day Martin Luther King Jr. arrested the consciousness of the world as he declared, "I have a dream." Within the course of his speech, these words flowed:

> In a sense we've come to our nation's capital to cash a check. When the architects of our republic wrote the magnificent words of the Constitution and the Declaration of Independence, they were signing a promissory note to which every American was to fall heir. This note was a promise that all men, yes, black men as well as white men, would be guaranteed the "unalienable Rights" of "Life, Liberty and the pursuit of Happiness."
>
> It is obvious today that America has defaulted on this promissory note, insofar as her citizens of color are

concerned. Instead of honoring this sacred obligation, America has given the Negro people a bad check, a check which has come back marked "insufficient funds."[1]

Fifty-seven years later, on August 28, 2020, many gathered again at the Mall with the check in hand still marked "insufficient funds." Fifty-seven years later, the signs that attendees held read the same. Fifty-seven years later, families of color mourned the loss of loved ones due to racial animus and indifference.

Consequently, we may ask, "Why keep trying to cash a check that bounces?" The answer is that the insufficiency of the funds does not cancel the legitimacy of the claim. America's inability to fully back the promissory note of freedom, justice, and equality for people of color does not lessen the validity of the claim nor the reasonableness of expectation. That is what Dr. King meant when he said:

We refuse to believe that the bank of justice is bankrupt. We refuse to believe that there are insufficient funds in the great vaults of opportunity of this nation. And so, we've come to cash this check, a check that will give us upon demand the riches of freedom and the security of justice.[2]

For people of faith, the historic and contemporary check bouncing does not quiet us. It prompts us to be even more forceful and determined in our demands. Our demands are grounded in something far greater than "enlightened humanity." Ours are grounded in sovereign expectations and demands of God Himself.

We cannot relax our demands because God has not relinquished His requirements. There is a consistency to what God requires. His requirements contain no sunset clause. They are not subject to reauthorization. They are neither diminished by time nor downgraded by the changing of political winds. They are not influenced by popular opinion or blunted by political correctness. God's requirements simply are.

God's Word reminds us of God's consistent requirements. The time of the Old Testament prophet Micah's ministry was a challenging one. It was filled with war between Judah and Assyria, with Judah paying heavy tributes to Assyria. Rulers and judges were on the take. Distrust and suspicion were predominant. Family institutions and dynamics were turned inside out and upside down. Sons dishonored fathers, and daughters rose up against mothers.

In the midst of widespread idolatry, fraud, theft, and corruption, certain prophets proclaimed words of peace for those who could pay, and the joys of wine and alcohol to those who would listen. Yet Micah emerged as one proclaiming the Lord's judgment:

Listen to what the LORD says:

"Stand up, plead my case before the mountains; let the hills hear what you have to say.

"Hear, you mountains, the LORD's accusation; listen, you everlasting foundations of the earth. For the LORD has a case against his people; he is lodging a charge against Israel.

"My people, what have I done to you? How have I burdened you? Answer me. I brought you up out of Egypt and redeemed you from the land of slavery. I sent Moses to lead you, also Aaron and Miriam. My people, remember what Balak king of Moab plotted and what Balaam son of Beor answered. Remember your journey from

Shittim to Gilgal, that you may know the righteous acts of the Lord."

With what shall I come before the Lord and bow down before the exalted God? Shall I come before him with burnt offerings, with calves a year old? Will the Lord be pleased with thousands of rams, with ten thousand rivers of olive oil? Shall I offer my firstborn for my transgression, the fruit of my body for the sin of my soul? He has shown you, O mortal, what is good. And what does the Lord require of you? To act justly and to love mercy and to walk humbly with your God. (Micah 6:1–8)

The charge in this chapter is that the people are acting inconsistently with the Lord's actions. Micah raises the Lord's faithfulness to the people in contradistinction to the people's faithfulness to the Lord.

With verse 6, Micah rhetorically raises questions about what the Lord requires in light of who He is and of how He's been to Israel. What pleases the Lord? And with what should we try to approach the Lord? Micah answers: "He has shown you . . ."

The word for *shown* means to put before, to place a matter high and conspicuous before a person. In other words, that which pleases God is not a secret. It's not hidden and obscure. God has openly and widely communicated and revealed it.

The word for *require* speaks to God seeking with care. It speaks to that which concerns God regarding us. God is carefully looking for certain things from us. The interests that God has for our lives, our living, our livelihood are what He requires of us. God's requirements are rooted in the care that He has for us. The requirements are never divorced from the concerns and desires God has. What God expects from us is always tied to what

He intends for us. Justice, mercy, and humility are matters He intends for us and desires to see from us.

God's First Requirement: Justice

From the very beginning, God openly shared His expectations and intentions. To the first humans, God said, "Be fruitful and increase in number; fill the earth and subdue it. Rule over the fish in the sea and the birds in the sky and over every living creature that moves on the ground. ... I give you every seed-bearing plant on the face of the whole earth and every tree that has fruit with seed in it. They will be yours for food" (Genesis 1:28–29).

Having planted Adam in Eden, God gave His requirements: "You are free to eat from any tree in the garden, but you must not eat from the tree of the knowledge of good and evil, for when you eat from it you will certainly die" (Genesis 2:16–17).

To Israel at Mount Sinai, God gave His requirements through Moses. In Deuteronomy 10:12: "What does the LORD your God ask of you but to fear the LORD your God, to walk in obedience to him, to love him, to serve the LORD your God with all your heart and with all your soul."

And now in Micah 6, we find three requirements: act justly, love mercy, and walk humbly with your God. The first two that Micah mentions are with reference to the people's duties toward one another. The third is how they are with God. The requirements God makes for our lives in community reflect what He desires us to experience in community. The first is "to act justly." In other translations, it reads, "do justice." The word for *justice* means judgment involved in determining rights and assigning rewards and punishments. Justice is one's entitlement under law. It is what each person should expect based upon what the law is. It is a commitment to fairness in interpersonal relationships, as well as in institutional engagement/involvement. Justice is the action or decision that vindicates or establishes the right.

The requirement and expectation of justice is never passive. It is active. That's why Micah does not say "talk justice," "sing justice," or "write justice." He says, "*do* justice," "*act* justly." The word for *do* means to make, to manufacture, to produce, to apply, to cause. Justice is something pursued, enacted, made, done, and applied. God's consistent requirement of and expectation for God's people is the doing and the experiencing of justice. Based upon God being God and of God delivering from that which was unjust—being Egyptian bondage—He demands and desires justice for His people in everything. The doing of justice is an expectation of and for everyone.

In Deuteronomy 10:17–19, God says, "For the LORD your God is God of gods and Lord of lords, the great, the mighty, and the awesome God, who is not partial and takes no bribe. He executes justice for the fatherless and the widow, and loves the sojourner, giving him food and clothing. Love the sojourner, therefore, for you were sojourners in the land of Egypt" (ESV).

Consequently, Israel's standards are expected to be just. In Leviticus 19:36, God speaks of requiring the Israelites to use just (honest) balances, just (honest) weights and measurements based upon the Lord bringing them out of Egypt. Proverbs 16:11 reads, "A just balance and scales are the LORD's" (ESV). Throughout the laws given to Moses, God fleshed out aspects of justice both in terms of what the Israelites should and should not do. They were to be impartial, shun bribes, and watch for the rights of the poor, the needy, the fatherless, and the afflicted. Even the psalms they sang reminded them of their responsibilities: "Give justice to the weak and the fatherless; maintain the right of the afflicted and the destitute" (Psalm 82:3, ESV).

This requirement, this expectation, is not just in the Old Testament. It is alive in the person and words of Jesus. In Luke 4:18–19, 21, Jesus began His ministry by reading the words of Isaiah:

"The Spirit of the Lord is on me, because he has anointed me to proclaim good news to the poor. He has sent me to proclaim freedom for the prisoners and recovery of sight for the blind, to set the oppressed free, to proclaim the year of the Lord's favor." . . . He began by saying to them, "Today this scripture is fulfilled in your hearing."

In Matthew 25:34–40, Jesus reasserted the required expectation:

The King will say to those on his right, "Come, you who are blessed by my Father; take your inheritance, the kingdom prepared for you since the creation of the world. For I was hungry and you gave me something to eat, I was thirsty and you gave me something to drink, I was a stranger and you invited me in, I needed clothes and you clothed me, I was sick and you looked after me, I was in prison and you came to visit me."

Then the righteous will answer him, "Lord, when did we see you hungry and feed you, or thirsty and give you something to drink? When did we see you a stranger and invited you in, or needing clothes and clothe you? When did we see you sick or in prison and go to visit you?"

The King will reply, "Truly I tell you, whatever you did for one of the least of these brothers and sisters of mine, you did for me." (NIV)

In Matthew 23:23, Jesus was even more pointed: "Woe to you, teachers of the law and Pharisees, you hypocrites! You tithe a tenth of your spices—mint, dill and cumin. But you have neglected the more important matters of the law—justice, mercy and faithfulness. You should have practiced the latter, without neglecting the former."

In today's terms, what might the requirement to "do justice" look like? Might it be to provide equal pay for equal work? Might it be to give equal interest rates for equal credit rating? Might it be offering equal and affordable access to quality health care? Might it be welcoming the stranger and mainstreaming the dreamers?

God's Second Requirement: Mercy

God's second requirement and expectation from and for us is that we "love mercy." We are called to desire, to delight in *chesed*, which is the Hebrew word for *mercy*, often translated as loyal love or covenant love. It speaks to the idea of faithfulness and loyalty within a covenant relationship. It alludes to the fulfillment of obligations to family, friends, and the community. *Chesed* involves God's undying love and loyalty to His people. It is an essential quality of God demonstrated by His faithfulness to His promises and to His commitment in relationship with His people, despite their unfaithfulness and disloyalty.

Jeremiah recognizes God's faithfulness to His promises and commitment in relationship to His people despite their faithlessness: "It is of the LORD's mercies that we are not consumed, because his compassions fail not. They are new every morning: great is thy faithfulness" (Lamentations 3:22–23, KJV). It is with this mercy that God calls on His people to love, to desire, to pursue, to chase after, and to long for. Mercy is the capacity to get inside another person's skin until we can see things with that person's eyes, think things with that person's mind, and feel things with that person's feelings. It is expressed as a goodness offered to someone when they can't help themselves and have nothing to offer in return. Mercy is what keeps you from experiencing the full consequences of your wrong, out of pity for you.

Having received God's mercy, Jesus in turn calls us to delight in showing that mercy to others. He encouraged us in Matthew 5:7, "Blessed are the merciful, for they will be shown mercy." Were it not for mercy, none of us would be able to stand alive. Therefore, in the midst of doing justice, God calls for us to love mercy. It is that love of mercy that brings humanity to do justice. It's that love of mercy that causes us to see the essential humanity in everyone, even in those who have done wrong. It's that love of mercy that keeps the victim from becoming a vigilante and victimizer. It's that love of mercy that puts restraint on anger and prevents anger from being destructive of ourselves and others. The love of mercy is what empowered Julia Jackson, Jacob Blake's mother, to say after her son had been shot seven times in the back by a police officer:

> My son has been fighting for his life, and we really just need prayers. As I was riding through here, through the city, I noticed a lot of damage. That doesn't reflect my son or my family. If Jacob knew what was going on, as far as that goes, the violence and the destruction, he would be very unpleased. . . . Do Jacob justice on this level and examine your hearts. We need healing. As I pray for my son's healing—physically, emotionally, and spiritually—I also have been praying, even before this, for the healing of our country.[3]

Doing justice and loving mercy are requirements and expectations that God has for us in respect to one another. We find an example of the two of them working in tandem in a story about a man caught and taken to court because he stole a loaf of bread.

When the judge investigated the man's situation, he found out that the man had no job, and his family was hungry. He had tried unsuccessfully to get work and finally, to feed his family, he stole the bread.

Although recognizing the extenuating circumstances, the judge said, "I'm sorry, but the law can make no exceptions. You stole, and therefore I have to punish you. I order you to pay a fine of ten dollars." He then continued, "But I want to pay the fine myself." The judge reached into his pocket, pulled out a ten-dollar bill, and handed it to the man. As soon as the man took the money, the judge said, "Now I also want to remit the fine." That is, the man could keep the money. "Furthermore, I am going to instruct the bailiff to pass around a hat to everyone in this courtroom, and I am fining everyone in this courtroom fifty cents for living in a city where a man has to steal in order to have bread to eat." The bailiff collected the money and handed it to the defendant.[4] This is an excellent example of justice being meted out in full and paid in full—while mercy and grace were also enacted in full measure. It is not enough to address the thievery. We must also address the structures and systems in a city that prohibit him from buying bread.

God's Third Requirement: Humility

The third requirement God has instituted for us is in respect to our relationship with Him. In reality, this third requirement serves as the foundation for us being able to consistently live out the first two. Our lives in community should be a reflection of our lives with God. The lives we live before the world are a manifestation of the lives we have or don't have with God.

Our lives with God empower and inform our lives with others. It is what God requires for life with Him that sets a conduit for what is necessary to do life with one another. We live with and before God in communion as we live with and before others in community. It is the life with and before God that should shape the life with and before each other. It is a God consciousness and sensitivity that enlivens the sensibilities we have for others. Thus Micah says, "Walk humbly with your God."

Far more important than offering money is that we offer our lives in relationship with God. We live that relationship characterized by humility. The life before God that informs the life before people is one of humility before God. That humility is recognizing and acknowledging who we are before God. Before God, we are limited. Before God, we are imperfect. Before God, we are lacking and insufficient. Before God, we are frail, vulnerable, mortal, corruptible. Before God, we are in constant need.

We need God for life, for health, for strength. We need God for wisdom, for knowledge, and for understanding. We need God for peace, for joy, for patience, for endurance. We need God to forgive, to cleanse, to make right. We need God for courage, for consistency. We need God's mercy and faithfulness. We are open to what He knows, what He sees, what He desires, what He has in mind. We are willing to put Him and His concerns above us and ours.

Walking humbly with and before God is acknowledging that there is a way that may seem right to humans, but its end leads only to destruction and death (see Proverbs 14:12). Walking humbly with God is trusting Him for direction in both the actions and in the outcomes. It's submitting to God by doing justice and showing mercy.

We Keep Presenting the Check

Justice, mercy, and humility are consistent requirements. That is why we never give up our pursuit for justice here in America. That is why we keep presenting the check to be cashed, regardless of how many times it bounces. That's what the generation of the Civil Rights Movement did. They marched and presented the check. They conducted sit-ins and presented the check. They boycotted and presented the check. They suffered beatings, jailings, bombings, and lynchings, presenting the check. They did so believing that sooner or later, justice would come. They kept presenting the check, believing that the God who requires and expects justice is the God who'll make the check good.

Though the moral arc of the universe be long, it bends toward justice, because God makes the check good. The God who requires justice is the God who is good for it. Sooner or later, He makes the check good.

Surely a degree of justice has come, but the debt is still outstanding. Too many checks have yet to be cashed. Too many promises of justice have yet to be kept. So we must keep on presenting the check, believing that sooner or later, justice must be done. Sooner or later, what is right and righteous must be established and experienced. Therefore, we don't give up. We keep presenting the check, because God makes the check good.

Moses presented the check to Pharaoh, who bounced the check. But he kept presenting it, and God made the check good. It took ten plagues and the Red Sea, but God made the check of deliverance and freedom good. He makes it good. He is good for it.

He made it good through Jesus. He came in the midst of injustice, marginalization, oppression, and discrimination. While subject to all of those, He did justice. He loved mercy. He walked humbly with God the Father.

When the Pharisees took a woman caught in the act of adultery to Jesus, they quoted the law and asked for His opinion. But He bent down and started to write in the sand and said, "Let any one of you who is without sin be the first to throw a stone at her"

(John 8:7). He didn't deny the facts. He just set forth the conditions of justice. The one without sin should cast the first stone.

One by one, the Pharisees left. With everyone else gone, Jesus was still there. He was without sin. He could cast the stone. Yet He had mercy. He told her, "Where are they? Has no one condemned you? . . . Then neither do I condemn you. . . . Go now and leave your life of sin" (John 8:10–11).

He did justice, He loved mercy, He walked humbly with God the Father. We see that humility in the garden of Gethsemane before He is arrested and ultimately crucified: "Not my will, but yours be done" (Luke 22:42). He acted in humility even in the face of an unfair and unjust trial. He did it for justice and mercy. He took the penalty of justice for us in order that we might experience the mercy of God through Him.

It is through Him that we do justice and love mercy. It is before Him that we walk looking for a change. We keep presenting the check believing that God will make it good. As the son of slaves, one of the founding fathers of American gospel music, Charles Albert Tindley wrote more than a century ago:

> Harder yet may be the fight;
> right may often yield to might;
> wickedness a while may reign;
> Satan's cause may seem to gain.
> But there's a God that rules above
> with hand of power and heart of love;
> and if I'm right, he'll fight my battle,
> I shall have peace someday.[5]

Part One

AWARENESS: HUMILITY REQUIRED

Chapter 5

COMING TO TERMS

Claude

The four-hundred-year history of race in America parallels the centuries- and, in some cases, millennia-long hostilities in many countries due to race, ethnicity, tribe, caste, and religion. Sadly, atrocities due to difference know no national or continental boundary. In far too many places in the world, the climate is skewing toward hostility. In an article titled "The Problem of Othering: Towards Inclusiveness and Belonging," John Powell and Stephen Menendian wrote:

> The problem of the twenty-first century is the problem of "othering." In a world beset by seemingly intractable and overwhelming challenges, virtually every global, national, and regional conflict is wrapped within or organized around one or more dimension of group-based difference. Othering undergirds territorial disputes, sectarian violence, military conflict, the spread of disease, hunger and food insecurity, and even climate change."[1]

These points of tension precede us. We have inherited them, some through the sheer coincidence of our births and others through a conscious decision to make Jesus our choice. While we do not bear responsibility for their origination, their continuation calls us to a level of ownership and responsibility, to becoming aware.

A Time of Multifaceted Responsibility

We are being called to a multifaceted time of responsibility and coming to terms. The first facet is historical. In America, we must come to terms with the dichotomy where men declared their independence and asserted their freedom while enslaving Africans and their descendants, and dispossessing indigenous Native Americans. We do so, recognizing that the transatlantic slave trade existed for 157 years prior to the Declaration of Independence. The matter of race and racism was the amniotic fluid into which many of the founders were born and would transmit as they gave birth to America as a nation.

Through a true historical awareness, we understand not just the historical reality, but also this contemporary moment, which is the second facet. America continues to have a dichotomy that is molecular in nature. The blessing/burden exists through biological inheritance and is reinforced through symbols, systems, structures, patterns, and behavior that operate with and without human intention. This realization of inherited blessings and burdens awakens us to certain contemporary realities and calls us into a responsibility to confront them.

Yet, it goes further than historical and contemporary. The denial of personhood, the denial of place, the denial of belonging that produces such historical and contemporary disparities is spiritual in nature, the third facet of awareness. That denial is an affront to the creative intention of God as demonstrated in the *imago Dei*. As such, the call for awareness and responsibility is not just historical and contemporary; it is also a spiritual awareness and responsibility we must take on, whereby we must confront sin, offer repentance, and experience redemption.

Whenever we speak of responsibility over the history of race and the continued existence of racism, some people will say, "Racism isn't my fault. I'm not racist. I have friends of color." I respond that it isn't my fault either. It is neither of our faults, but it *is* something that exists for which God calls us to own and change. None of us chose the race to which we were born. God assigned and designed it to us. With its conferral came blessings and burdens that we inherit. Thus, while the existence of racism, prejudice, and bigotry is not our fault, it is our problem. We all must own it as our problem. While we may not bear responsibility for its commencement, we do have responsibility in its continuance.

We must become aware and take responsibility with and own what wasn't our fault as still being our problem. We must come to terms with experiencing the consequences of what we didn't create ourselves. This is a serious challenge. We have to live under the weight of what was begun by someone else.

The prophet Daniel helps us come to terms with how that responsibility looks.

Lessons from the Prophet Daniel

For sixty-six years, Daniel and his people lived under the reign of foreign and idolatrous regimes. Beginning with Nebuchadnezzar of Babylon and then Darius of Mede, they were kept from their homeland. Finally during the first year of Darius' reign, an awareness rose within Daniel. That awareness opened Daniel's eyes to the reality that the upheaval he and his people were experiencing was not just political. There was more going on than just political machination and maneuvering.

In his search for an answer, Daniel looked to the Scriptures—in particular, to Jeremiah's prophecies. In Jeremiah 25:8–12, he found:

> The LORD Almighty says this: "Because you have not listened to my words, I will summon all the peoples of the north and my servant Nebuchadnezzar king of Babylon . . . and I will bring them against this land and its inhabitants and against all the surrounding nations. I will completely destroy them and make them an object of horror and scorn, and an everlasting ruin. I will banish from them the sounds of joy and gladness, the voices of bride and bridegroom, the sound of millstones and the light of the lamp. This whole country will become a desolate wasteland, and these nations will serve the king of Babylon seventy years.
>
> "But when the seventy years are fulfilled, I will punish the king of Babylon and his nation, the land of the Babylonians, for their guilt . . . and I will make it desolate forever."

He also read Jeremiah 29:10–14:

> This is what the LORD says: "When seventy years are completed for Babylon, I will come to you and fulfill my good promise to bring you back to this place. For I know the plans I have for you," declares the LORD, "plans to prosper you and not to harm you, plans to give you hope and a future. Then you will call on me and come and pray to me, and I will listen to you. You will seek me and find me when you seek me with all your heart. I will be found by you . . . and will bring you back from captivity."

In reading the Word of the Lord, Daniel said that he learned. Those Scriptures given for our instruction and learning were also the historical record for Daniel about his people. He did not read merely as a devotional exercise. He read to discern a historical and contemporary locating of himself. As he sought to better understand where he currently was, he sought the Scriptures, which gave him historical and spiritual understanding. In reading them, he learned. He absorbed. He took in. He came to understand.

The awareness was a call to understand the present in light of the past. Daniel came to better understand where he was in light of his people's distant and recent histories. He recalled why they were taken to Babylon in the first place: as a result of God's judgment upon their sin. The people's sinfulness resulted in their coming under God's judgment and their subsequent exile in Babylon. The people's failure to follow God's ways and to heed the warnings of the prophets before them set the stage for the exile that they were forced to endure. Daniel had been in Babylon for sixty-six years, due to the sins of his ancestors. He was suffering the results of someone else's wrongs. He was paying the price for the faults of a preceding generation. Though he lived a life of integrity, honoring God in his choices, he still suffered the exile and captivity.

This suffering produced a conflict within him, because he had to bear results from what weren't his actions. Understanding that the history of his people was not just natural but also spiritual, and that his life was also spiritual, he responded spiritually:

I turned to the Lord God and pleaded with him in prayer and petition, in fasting, and in sackcloth and ashes.

I prayed to the LORD my God and confessed:

"Lord, the great and awesome God, who keeps his covenant of love with those who love him and keep his commandments, we have sinned and done wrong. We have been wicked and rebelled; we have turned away from your commands and laws. We have not listened to your servants the prophets, who spoke in your name to our kings, our princes and our ancestors, and to all the people of the land.

"Lord, you are righteous, but this day we are covered with shame—the people of Judah and the inhabitants of Jerusalem and all Israel, both near and far, in all the countries where you have scattered us because of our unfaithfulness to you. We and our kings, our princes and our ancestors are covered with shame, LORD, because we have sinned against you." (Daniel 9:3–8)

The awareness is where we come to terms with our personal responsibility. True awareness reminds us that we are not faultless. As Daniel contemplated this situation both as it related to its cause in the distant past and to its contemporary reality, he fought against pride and self-righteousness. Self-righteous indignation would rise up within Daniel and cause him to pray a different prayer. Rather than saying, "We have sinned," Daniel would have said, "They have sinned." It would be so easy to make it a matter of *them*. His pride would cause him to reject the notion that their circumstances had anything to do with him.

Looking Inward

Rather than continuing to look outwardly at others, Daniel looked inwardly at himself. In this self-reflection, he did not look at himself in comparison with others. He did not examine himself in comparison to the generation that provoked God's judgment. He looked at himself in comparison to God. Let's look again at Daniel 9:4–5 where he prayed:

Lord, the great and awesome God, who keeps his covenant of love with those who love him and keep his commandments, we have sinned and done wrong.

As he looked inwardly in light of the person of God, Daniel saw his shortcomings. He saw his failures. He saw his faults. He was touched by his condition. He was sorrowful for himself. He was humbled by what he saw in himself. Therefore, rather than lifting himself above others, he saw himself in the same boat. And he confessed and repented: "I went on praying and confessing my sin and the sin of my people" (Daniel 9:20, NLT).

Authentic awareness, where we don't just look at what was and is but we look at it in light of who God is and what God demands, is one where we recognize that we are not faultless. It forces us to come to terms with where we are currently. While we aren't not responsible for where we've been, we *are* responsible for where we are. Where we are is a reflection of our decision and indecision. Where we are is a reflection of our compromises and complicity. Where we are is a reflection of our aggression and passivity, our engagement and detachment, our courage and our cowardice. Whenever that happens, it is no longer what "they" did. We must fess up to what "we've" done. We must own what we've allowed, where we've compromised, where we've been culpable, where we've been cowardly . . .

Awareness that Leads to Humility

Daniel humbled himself and prayed a prayer of confession, not just because he realized he was not without fault but also because he was concerned about making things right.

The awareness motivates a focus on how to make things right. Daniel understood he had a choice to make. With every right to be bitter, Daniel could spend his time blaming, but that wouldn't change the situation. He began to focus on how he could make things right. Even though he had nothing to do with the reason for their being in exile, he would be a part of its solution.

Having searched the Scriptures, Daniel knew that they had been exiled due to God's judgment upon the people's sin. He also knew that God set the time of that judgment to be seventy years. He further knew that they had been in exile for sixty-six years. The question became, *When the people reach the seventieth year, will we have done what we needed to do?* He was mindful of Leviticus 26:

> If in spite of this you still do not listen to me but continue to be hostile toward me, then in my anger I will be hostile toward you, and I myself will punish you for your sins seven times over. . . . I will turn your cities into ruins and lay waste your sanctuaries, and I will take no delight in the pleasing aroma of your offerings. I myself will lay waste the land, so that your enemies who live there will be appalled. I will scatter you among the nations and will draw out my sword and pursue you. (vv. 27–28, 31–33)

Yet, the Lord offers a turn:

> But if they will confess their sins and the sins of their ancestors—their unfaithfulness and their hostility toward me, which made me hostile toward them so that I sent them into the land of their enemies—then when their uncircumcised hearts are humbled and they pay for their sin, I will remember my covenant with Jacob and my covenant with Isaac and my covenant with Abraham, and I will remember the land." (vv. 40–42)

Daniel recognized that God was just and righteous. God was just in disciplining Israel for their sins. He recognized that God was keeping His word. In the Scriptures, Daniel found what he needed to do to help make things right. If God was faithful and just to do what He promised in response to their sin, then He must be faithful and just to do what He said in response to their repentance. With the people's failure to repent and to confess, Daniel took the responsibility upon himself to repent and confess on behalf of the people. He didn't put them into the mess, but he would do what he could to get them out.

He would say, "Listen as I plead. . . . O my God, lean down and listen to me. Open your eyes and see our despair. . . . O Lord, hear. O Lord, forgive. O Lord, listen and act! For your own sake, do not delay" (Daniel 9:17–19, NLT).

Daniel showed that we may not have been the one who created the issue, but we can be the one who helps correct it. We've got two choices: spending our time blaming and faultfinding or doing what we can to make things right. The question before us is, "Who's going to do what needs to be done to correct it?"

What will you do to make things better, to make things right? Daniel recognized that it might not have been his fault, but it was his opportunity to do what he could to make things better. While Daniel was still praying and confessing, God sent the archangel Gabriel to give him a word of understanding and encouragement. The city's transgression would be finished. An end to sin would be made. Atonement for wickedness would be provided. Everlasting righteousness would be brought. Jerusalem would be restored and rebuilt.

When you rise up to the responsibility, God will give you what you need in the midst of it. He'll give you a word. He'll give you a vision. He'll give you a promise. He'll give you what you need to correct it, to change it, to fix it, to redeem it, or to save it.

No, we didn't start the tensions and challenges in our cities and nations, but we can be agents of correction, transformation, and redemption. After all, isn't that what God did for us in Christ? He looked beyond our faults and saw our need for a savior. He sent Jesus into the world. Jesus came into a situation that wasn't His fault. The fall of humanity wasn't His fault. The fault was Adam's. The fault was mine. The fault was yours. But Jesus entered the mess we made. Even though He didn't create it, He came to correct it. He came to redeem it. He who knew no sin became sin for us that we might be made the righteousness of God through Him (2 Corinthians 5:21).

Jesus calls us to awareness and responsibility in our cities, our countries, and indeed the world. In truth, we have a far more compelling reality and experience to present the world. It is the kingdom of God.

Chapter 6

A NECESSARY CONVERSATION

Claude

I have always been fascinated by John's depiction of Jesus in chapter 4: "He left Judea and went back once more to Galilee. Now he had to go through Samaria. So he came to a town in Samaria called Sychar, near the plot of ground Jacob had given to his son Joseph" (vv. 3–5). Jesus had to go through what others would usually avoid because of the racial tension that existed.

The term *Samaritan*, for the Jew, was a pejorative term, akin to the "N" word today. It applied to the racial identity of those Jews who intermarried with Assyrians during and after the Assyrian invasion. Subsequently, they were denied a place in rebuilding the temple and of worship in Jerusalem. When traveling from Galilee to Judah or vice versa, every upstanding Jewish person would travel around it rather than go through it. In fact, there were times when Jesus even went around it rather than through it. But on this occasion, He "had to go through" what He would normally go around.

As Jesus arrived in Samaria, He met a Samaritan woman, who was drawing water during the hottest part of the day. She did so because her lifestyle put her at odds with the other women of the city. Jesus engaged her in a way that altered her life to such a degree that she returned to the city bearing witness to Him. It caused the townspeople to go see and hear Him for themselves. As a result, many came to faith in Him. By going into Samaria rather than around it, and by engaging someone whom others shunned, Jesus connected with one whom God used to evangelize the whole city.

In Acts 1 when Jesus spoke of the disciples receiving power from the Holy Spirit coming upon them and of their being witnesses unto Him, He intentionally included Samaria as a place of witnessing. By that inclusion, He was telling them that they must confront the place of racial tension for the furtherance of the gospel. They could not avoid or ignore it. If their gospel witness was to have its intended impact, they must go there.

Confronting this place of racial tension is the greatest challenge of the American church. We don't do Samaria well. We are more comfortable with the outermost parts of the earth than we are with America's Samaria. Yet if our gospel witness is to have its intended impact, we must go there. We cannot avoid or ignore it. And it starts with an unavoidable and necessary conversation.

Where Do We Begin?

What do the following cities have in common: Atlanta; Baltimore; Baton Rouge; Bensonhurst, Brooklyn; Birmingham; Boston; Charleston; Charlotte; Chicago; Cleveland; Colfax, Louisiana; Detroit; East St. Louis; Ferguson, Missouri; Gary; Greensboro; Jackson, Mississippi; Kirven, Texas; Knoxville; Long Island; Longview, Texas; Los Angeles; Memphis; Miami; Minneapolis; Montgomery; Newark; New Orleans; New York; Omaha; Philadelphia; Queens; Rosewood, Florida; Sanford, Florida; Selma; Tulsa; Washington, DC; and Watts?

The answer? They are all cities that experienced racial strife and progress.

The reality is that every city in America has been touched by the issue of race. Consider the composition, design, and amenities of neighborhoods. Think about where schools are placed, populated, and maintained. Look at where city architects site utility and sanitation plants. Even major highways cutting through neighborhoods and the location of airports all are often tracked by economics, and those poorer populations tend to align by race.

Throughout history, institutional structures and practices of city-community life—including codes, customs, and policies—have revealed and reinforced the vision and value of racial inequality or equality. Whether intentional or unintentional, consciously and unconsciously, our cities-communities have often made choices, actions, and reactions that are informed, influenced, and impacted by race. Those choices, actions, and reactions then consequently have the ability to provide or deny access, inclusion, or justice to their citizens. And throughout history, in each city-community, there have been churches whose activity or passivity have positively or negatively responded.

If we want any gospel-centered city movement to have integrity and relevance, then we must confront the matter of race.

So where do we begin? We begin by accepting that this is a necessary discussion for the church, because we understand that the nature of the problem is spiritual, for which we are uniquely equipped to speak both in terms of repentance—for the role the church has actively and passively played in the problem of race—and in recognition of the prophetic role the church has played in the struggle against racism.

Ignorance is not bliss, and we cannot speak well to something we don't know and understand enough about. So we begin by gaining a better understanding of the historical and contemporary facts and forces of racism in America. If we are to be agents of reconciliation—which God calls us to be—we must know that reconciliation entails recognition of the break in its depth and severity. It is anchored in the historical realities of the break in relationship, in the historical offense. Reconciliation cannot be some amorphous wish that ignores, avoids, downplays, or discounts the actual wounding event(s).

That is where we begin. By becoming aware.

The Roots of the Relationship Break

The majority of us were either undereducated or miseducated in the history of race in America. Before the Pilgrims arrived on the Mayflower, 113 years before the birth of George Washington, and 157 years before the Declaration of Independence and our birth as a nation, slaves arrived on our shores. Often viewed as the product of the South, the enslavement of Africans in America was actually legalized first in Massachusetts in 1641. New laws separating Black slaves from European indentured servants began to appear in 1676. Slavery became permanent and heritable for "Negroes." Poor Whites could become empowered by serving as overseers who policed the slaves. More pointedly, as slavery became associated with blackness, the emergence of the term *White* began appearing in both legal code and social custom. As early as 1706, slave codes began to be passed in both the Northern and Southern colonies to solidify the legalization of the enslavement of Blacks.[1]

By the time of the Constitutional Convention of 1787, in order to keep the young country united, the Constitution's framers accommodated the Southern colonies by allowing the Three-Fifths Compromise, over which African slaves were designated as three-fifths human for the purposes of establishing the number of representatives a state may have, as well as the way taxes would be levied and collected. In short, the Africans and their descendants were human enough to count for the number of representatives a state may have and less than human enough to be property subject to taxation, trading, insuring, mortgaging, and inheriting.[2]

This was followed by the Naturalization Act of 1790 that reserved citizenship for Whites only. The denial of citizenship prohibited non-Whites from voting, owning property, bringing suit, and testifying in court. It wouldn't be until 1868, with the Fourteenth Amendment, that African Americans would be guaranteed citizenship. Groups of Native Americans would become citizens through individual treaties or intermarriage, until 1924 with the passing of the Indian Citizenship Act. Asian immigrants were denied citizenship until 1954, with the McCarran-Walter Act, which removed all racial barriers to naturalization.[3]

Expanding Slavery and Racism

We are often prone to view America's history of racism being a matter of the South. However, with the country's expansion to the West, southerners took the institution of slavery westward.

What is now Arizona was originally part of the New Mexico Territory. When the Southern states seceded from the Union, the Confederate States of America broke apart the New Mexico Territory to form the Territory of Arizona.[4]

While disapproving of slavery, in 1857 Oregon incorporated into its Bill of Rights a clause that prohibited Blacks from being in the state, owning property, and making contracts. This made Oregon the only state to enter the Union with a Black exclusion law in its constitution.[5]

In 1854, in People v. Hall, the California Supreme Court reversed the conviction of a White man in a murder trial, ruling that the testimony of "key Chinese witnesses is inadmissible," because "no Black or Mulatto person, or Indian, shall be allowed to give evidence in favor of, or against a white man." The rationale of the Chief Justice is telling. He claimed that the Chinese are "a race of people whom nature has marked as inferior, and who are incapable of progress or intellectual development beyond a certain point. . . . The same rule which would admit them to testify, would admit them to all the equal rights of citizenship, and we might soon see them at the polls, in the jury box, upon the bench, and in our legislative halls. This is not a speculation . . . but it is an actual and present danger."[6]

The US Supreme Court's Dred Scott decision of 1857 upheld the Fugitive Slave Act, reasserting that neither free nor enslaved Blacks were citizens. While free Black people were taxed like Whites, they did not enjoy the same protections and entitlements. When slaves in Washington, DC, were freed in 1862, the only reparation paid was to slaveowners for the loss of their property.[7]

While President Lincoln's Emancipation Proclamation of 1863 legally outlawed slavery in Texas and the Confederate states, the enforcement of it in Texas did not occur until June 19, 1865 (Juneteenth)—more than two years after emancipation and a full two months after the end of the Civil War—when General Gordon Grainger, accompanied by a Union Army, proclaimed freedom for slaves.[8]

Even with the proclamation reaching Texas on June 19, slavery was still legally practiced in Delaware and Kentucky until the Thirteenth Amendment was ratified on December 6, 1865. While the Thirteenth Amendment abolished chattel slavery nationwide in 1865, it wouldn't be until a year later in 1866 when the Choctaw and Chickasaw Indians signed a treaty with the United States, which forced them to release those who were enslaved.[9]

Though the Fourteenth Amendment (1868) granted citizenship to all persons born or naturalized in the United States, including formerly enslaved people, and guaranteed equal protection under the law, and the Fifteenth Amendment (1870) granted African-American men the right to vote, so-called Black Codes, which sought to control the labor and behavior of freed slaves and placed poll taxes on Black voters, practically denied Blacks the full rights of citizenship.

More Freedom and Opportunities Denied

This Southern retrenchment that sought to relegate the newly freed Blacks to second-class citizenship was known as Jim Crow. Dr. David Pilgrim, professor of sociology at Ferris State University, described Jim Crow:

> The Jim Crow system was undergirded by the following beliefs or rationalizations: whites were superior to blacks in all important ways, including but not limited to intelligence, morality, and civilized behavior; sexual relations between blacks and whites would produce a mongrel race which would destroy America; treating blacks as equals would encourage interracial sexual unions; any activity which suggested social equality encouraged interracial sexual relations; if necessary, violence must be used to keep blacks at the bottom of the racial hierarchy. The following Jim Crow etiquette norms show how inclusive and pervasive these norms were:
>
> - A black male could not offer his hand (to shake hands) with a white male because it implied being socially equal. Obviously, a black male could not offer his hand or any other part of his body to a white woman, because he risked being accused of rape.

- Blacks and whites were not supposed to eat together. If they did eat together, whites were to be served first, and some sort of partition was to be placed between them. . . .
- Blacks were not allowed to show public affection toward one another in public, especially kissing, because it offended whites. . . .
- Whites did not use courtesy titles of respect when referring to blacks, for example, Mr., Mrs., Miss., Sir, or Ma'am. Instead, blacks were called by their first names. Blacks had to use courtesy titles when referring to whites, and were not allowed to call them by their first names.
- If a black person rode in a car driven by a white person, the black person sat in the back seat, or the back of a truck.
- White motorists had the right-of-way at all intersections.[10]

These norms were reinforced by state laws that regulated social interaction and established the segregation of public accommodations, schools, hospitals, prisons, cemeteries, restrooms, water fountains, and entrances. White paramilitary groups such as the Red Shirts, the White League, state Democratic Rifle Clubs, and the Ku Klux Klan enforced the Jim Crow system through violence in the form of lynchings, shootings, and house burnings. The US Supreme Court added its voice by upholding Jim Crow segregation laws for public facilities in its 1896 Plessy v. Ferguson decision. It is with this decision that we got the doctrine of "separate but equal."[11]

Racial segregation was not limited to the actions of states and courts. The federal government adopted segregation under

President Woodrow Wilson in 1913 and did not integrate until the 1960s. This posture was seen in a number of policies at the federal level. The three most glaring examples are in housing, the Social Security Act, and the GI Bill. As the federal government began to create programs that subsidized low-cost loans for housing in the 1930s and 1940s, government underwriters introduced a national appraisal system that tied property value and loan eligibility to race, creating what we know as "redlining." All-White communities received the highest ratings and benefited from low-cost, government-backed loans. Minority and mixed neighborhoods received the lowest ratings and were denied such loans. Estimates suggest that out of the $120 billion worth of new housing subsidized between 1934 and 1962, less than 2 percent went to non-White families. This redlining was buttressed by restrictive covenants that prohibited homeowners from selling or leasing their homes to non-Whites.

In 1935, the Social Security Act was passed and exempted agricultural workers and domestic servants (predominantly African American, Mexican, and Asian) from receiving old-age insurance, while the Wagner Act guaranteed workers' rights but did not prohibit unions from discriminating against non-Whites. This resulted in non-Whites being denied higher-paying jobs and union benefits, such as medical care, full employment, and job security.

Perhaps the most glaring example of systemic racism in federal government policy is the GI Bill of 1944, which was enacted to help returning veterans from World War II by establishing hospitals, low-interest mortgages, and stipends to cover tuition and expenses for college and trade schools. It also included low-interest loans to start a business, one year of unemployment compensation, and low-interest, zero-down-payment home loans. From 1944 to 1949, nearly 9 million veterans received close to $4 billion from the bill's unemployment compensation program. All of which was to the exclusion of non-Whites.[12]

As more White homeowners moved to the suburbs in the 1950s and 1960s, federal and state tax dollars subsidized the construction and development of infrastructure, which incented commercial investment. Freeways in major cities were built to connect White suburbs to the center city, often at the cost of disrupting and dividing thriving Black neighborhoods. In the city of Charlotte, Interstates 77 and 85 were cut between two Black neighborhoods and even divided a Black cemetery. This resulted in neighborhoods losing shopping districts and many successful businesses closing.

Judicial Changes Come

In 1954, the United States began to see a change at the judicial level. In the Brown v. Board of Education of Topeka decision, the Supreme Court declared state laws establishing separate public schools for Black and White students to be unconstitutional, overturning Plessy v. Ferguson. De jure (legal) racial segregation was ruled a violation of the Equal Protection Clause of the Fourteenth Amendment and set the context for integration.[13]

Between 1964 and 1968, Congress passed several signal pieces of legislation. In 1964, they passed the Civil Rights Act, which outlawed discrimination based on race, color, religion, sex, or national origin, ending unequal application of voter registration requirements and racial segregation in schools, at the workplace, and in public accommodations. This was followed by the Voting Rights Act of 1965, which prohibited racial discrimination in voting. Finally, the Fair Housing Act was passed in 1968, outlawing discrimination concerning the sale, rental, and financing of housing based on race, religion, national origin, and sex.[14]

Letting Our Awareness Lead to Understanding

I have provided this brief anchoring in history to give us a cursory understanding of the facts and forces that shape the contemporary realities we face. My hope is that it awakens us to the fact that what we currently face in our cities is because of what is in the historical and structural fabric of our cities. We can't have a four-hundred-year history of structural and systemic racial injustice and inequality and expect all the remnants and consequences to disappear in fifty years. Some stuff is simply in the ground. It's what Pete Scazzero, author of *The Emotionally Healthy Church*, would suggest is in the bones.

In the conclusion to Barna's study "Beyond Diversity," the authors quote David Bailey, founder of Arrabon, offering the following metaphor to help people understand the individual and systemic issues:

In America, the law has been established for about 100 years that we have to drive our cars on the right side of the road. If that law were to be reversed immediately today, would our thoughts, attitudes and behaviors change as quickly as the law? How many years do you think it would take before our bias to drive on the right side of the road would change?

Having people shift from driving from the right side of the road to the left side of the road isn't just a matter of changing people's thoughts, attitudes and actions. There were structures in place to reinforce the thought that driving on the right side of the road is appropriate and normal. Think about all of the systems of traffic lights, signs, road patterns and even vehicle design that would have to be dismantled and new systems that would have to be put into place to support a "new normal." Think about how many generations it would take before society was fully rid of the habits and symbols of the old driving system.

Our country has been organized around (and divided by) race for 350 years, and even as laws and social norms continue to evolve to make racism less acceptable, we have not gone through a transformation in our thoughts, attitudes and actions. We have not finished removing the systems associated with old behaviors and setting up new ones. We have racial biases that we need to be aware of and discipled out of.[15]

Just as a physician seeks to get a family history to better understand the particular pathology that might be alive in you, so is understanding the history of race in our nation and in our cities crucial to understanding the pathology that we see. While it is true that the blood of Jesus has power over everything, part of the power of the blood is its ability to address matters in their specificity and not simply in their generality.

Chapter 7

MOVEMENT DAY 757: FROM AWARENESS TO TRANSFORMATION

Mac

The cities of the Hampton Roads region in Virginia are facing dual challenges. The first challenge is the disparity of economics and opportunity between many of the African-American and White communities. The second challenge is the racial division within the church of Jesus Christ.

One of these economic crises is affordable housing. According to the Legal Aid Society of Eastern Virginia, Norfolk is preparing to close three public-housing communities located in the St. Paul's region. This closure will dislocate nearly 4,200 people, including 2,000 children. As of April 30, 2021, with no real affordable options, residents leaving the public housing still had nowhere to go.[1] In addition, food insecurity impacts one in ten families in this region, representing more than 180,000 people.[2]

That's housing and food. Let's consider education. According to the National Center for Education Statistics, across the state of Virginia, African-American children are twenty-five points behind White students for fourth-grade reading scores.[3] Only 19 percent of African-American students in Virginia are considered proficient.[4] Children who are unable to read at grade level by the fourth grade are four times less likely to graduate high school. For children in poorer communities, they are six times less likely to graduate.[5]

The correlation between underperforming reading and incarceration rates is equally stunning. According to Northeastern University researchers, high-school dropouts are sixty-three times more likely to be incarcerated than college graduates.[6]

This crisis didn't just happen overnight. Decades of disadvantage have created this environment. While government and local communities have not done enough to address these realities to make lasting, positive change, unfortunately, neither has the church. A divided church in the midst of a divided society has crippled many of the efforts of Christians to make a redemptive difference in cities. And yet churches and Christian agencies are waking up and becoming more aware. After several years of seed sowing from 2011 to 2016, a group of Virginia churches and agencies across the racial spectrum formed an alliance to address these issues head on, eager to make a difference together. This alliance is called the "757," and they are Movement Day Virginia Cities (MDVC).

Forming A New Community

From 2011 through 2016, Travis Simone, pastor of the Williamsburg Chapel, along with his father, Michael, attended each year's Movement Day in New York City. Travis had been so impacted by his experience at Movement Day that he spent a year preaching on the theme of gospel movement at his church. He also began gathering leaders at luncheons to cast vision and discuss the needs of their region.

One member of those luncheon gatherings was Clif Brigham, an accountant and elder at the Chapel. He hosted gatherings in his home to introduce the impact of Movement Day to his network. What emerged was a biracial core group of Clif, Andy Cronan (an architect), Charlie Williams (a marketing executive), and Mike Morse (a physician). From his home, they moved their gathering to Fridays at First Baptist Church of Williamsburg, pastored by Dr. Reginald Davis—one of the oldest African-American churches in the nation—to pray.

One day Eric Thompson and Andy Cronan met at a bridal shower of Andy's nephew and Eric's great niece. This meeting resulted in Andy introducing Eric to Movement Day and led them to attend the first Movement Day in Charlotte in 2018. Eric, a senior wealth manager at UBS, had been convening leaders in his own series of luncheons. He was involved in a biracial prayer meeting which met at Gethsemane Community Fellowship. And he was convinced that Norfolk was ready for such an effort.

And what became known as Movement Day Virginia Cities (MDVC), or the 757, was birthed. The 757 is takes its name from the 757 area code of Norfolk, Williamsburg, Hampton, Virginia Beach, Chesapeake, Newport News, Portsmouth, and Suffolk. It is comprised of a core group of forty leaders who meet to foster unity in the body of Christ toward spiritual and social flourishing. They are also committed to bridging four divides: racial, economic, denominational, and geographic.

Pastor Travis Simone hosted a luncheon in June 2016 in Williamsburg, with twenty-five leaders gathering. Later that year, they attended Movement Day Global Cities in New York City and returned "home" ready to discuss its impact on them and how they could use what they experienced to jumpstart their own Movement Day experiences. For the next two years, they met with emerging stakeholders to establish the first MDVC event in 2019.

By 2019, they were ready. A wonderfully diverse group gathered in Norfolk, Williamsburg, and Newport News, including civic leaders (the mayor of Norfolk), church leaders, community/nonprofit leaders, and commerce/marketplace leaders across the region.

They brought Claude and me to speak and to see what was happening in their region. Because 2019 held significance as the four-hundredth anniversary of when the first slaves were brought to America at Jamestown, the 757 took that opportunity for their MDVC to remember the impact of slavery on African Americans, and to bring diverse churches together to address contemporary challenges. As the movement has matured, the group has entered into more in-depth discussions to deepen their unity and mobilize effective action.

During that Movement Day gathering, they decided to form "design teams" that were responsible to study and strategize toward the great needs of their communities that were most challenged. These teams went straight to work, meeting immediately and planning practical ways to impact their communities.

The COVID-19 pandemic that hit the globe in 2020 didn't slow down the 757. Eric Thompson, Andy Cronan, Charlie Williams, and Clif Brigham helped establish a weekly Zoom group, with Veronica Thomas, pastor of First United Presbyterian Church in Norfolk, and Richard Young, vice president of ArcaMax Publishing from Newport News, as core members. On February 29, of that year, the MDVC community began weekly Zoom calls and continued to birth several working groups. The group, comprised of thirty to forty African-American and White leaders, meet every Saturday, except for holidays, and are ferociously loyal to one another and to their purpose. As of this book's writing, the group has now met more than seventy consecutive weeks.

"The 757 weekly call has been a blessing in bringing fellow believers together," says Pastor Rob Whitehead of New Zion Baptist Church in Williamsburg. "It allowed men and women, whose paths would not ordinarily cross, to come together, listen, learn, and discern, as we've sought to maneuver in a new situation. I think the call set the stage for an open environment when the political and social climates were not always positive in the nation. The call is a reminder that we can overcome some things when Christ is first."

In the past two years, following the first MDVC, they have made early-stage strides tackling issues of spiritual poverty, food insecurity, education inequality, and housing challenges. And they continue to use Movement Day gatherings as a vehicle to pray, educate, and mobilize leaders into thoughtful engagement. They are building a solid alliance.

Building an Alliance

The foundation of the alliance is prayer. Members spend time praying together in the different cities and on their weekly Zoom calls. It is during these prayer times that the 757's diverse leaders have built strong relationships and forged trust as they pray for one another and the needs of their communities.

The weekly Zoom calls begin with a presentation on a monthly theme (such as education, housing, unity, Bible poverty). They follow with the leaders breaking off into small groups of four and praying together for fifteen to twenty minutes. While the group averages forty members participating weekly, the 757 calls have had more than two hundred different leaders join, with their peak gathering of eighty leaders on one Zoom call to hear about an economic initiative.

In addition to the Zoom calls, local churches have participated in biracial B CARE groups (Biblical Conversations About

Race and Ethnicity). The B CARE pilot, formed in September 2020, took two groups through six weekly sessions in which they studied John Perkins' *One Blood: Parting Words to the Church on Race and Love*.[7] The final week included testimonies and a celebration. The initial churches were Williamsburg Chapel (one of the larger Protestant churches in Williamsburg) and Mount Pleasant Baptist Church. With the pilot's success of "graduating" forty-six participants, the 757 decided to launch two new groups each fall and two more in the spring.

The impact of the study has been an awakening of Christians to the strong theme of cultural understanding in the Bible and its centrality, and it has helped White Christians better understand the cultural experiences of their African-American brothers and sisters. Chapel's associate pastor, Dale South, and outreach director, Elizabeth Duncan, organized this B CARE initiative with the support of Enid Butler and Rubin Eatmon. They wanted to make it a Movement initiative so that it would not be owned by one church.

Claire Jacobs, one of the B CARE outreach directors, said that her involvement has resulted, for the first time in her life, in having an extended conversation one-on-one with an African-American woman. Elizabeth Duncan, mission director at Williamsburg Chapel, admitted that her involvement has allowed her to get outside of her racial bubble. And Enid Butler, who helped design the B CARE groups and train facilitators, expressed gratitude for the ways the group and the 757 has allowed her to practically engage the needs of the community.

In addition to the B CARE groups, other events, such as the March for Jesus, have brought the community together to visibly demonstrate the relationships between different faith communities. It has been important to get the church out of its own walls.

Other 757 members have pursued different opportunities as well, with MDVC providing a conduit for both volunteers and funding to accelerate the work. One example was Reverends Eric "Duke" and Linda "Duchess" McCaskill, who had earlier founded Alpha and Omega Network, which launched PACCT, the Police and Concerned Citizens Together alliance. In describing its mission, one journalist summarized it as "handshakes, conversation, and bags of food: police building relationships with residents of Aqueduct Apartments."[8] The Aqueduct Apartments are associated with low income and crime, "a homicide hotspot."

Another initiative is called "Police Presence with Presents." National chains including Chick-fil-A and Texas Roadhouse provide a catered meal while the police provide toys to children. More recently the police have assisted in providing food distribution during this season of food insecurity. In this initiative both police and local ministers go door to door providing food and expressions of support.

According to Duke, "The interaction between the police officers and African-American citizens changes negative perceptions into positive realities. This is how Black lives can be saved." Part of PACCT's mission, according to Duke—who also helped integrate Purdue University during his student years and as a track athlete—is to align these efforts with teaching virtues to young people. For their leadership in the community, Eric and Linda received honorary doctorate degrees from Providence Bible College and Theological Seminary.

Turning Meetings to Action

The leaders within the 757 don't only engage in meetings, they put their prayers to action—feeding the hungry, building literacy rates, tackling homelessness, managing business incubation, and addressing spiritual poverty.

Feeding the Hungry

Food insecurity became an increasing need during the COVID-19 pandemic. Many medium- and low-skilled workers lost their livelihoods due to business shutdowns. As the result of the 757's work, leaders were able to coordinate to deliver eighteen thousand pounds of food every month across seven locations, including Norfolk, Virginia Beach, Williamsburg, and Newport News.

The food security ecosystem was radically impacted by the group meeting on Zoom every week. Leadership for this effort included local churches, area food banks, the NAACP, and the Christian Broadcast Network. Mary Bibbs, from Bibbs Firm LLC, and Deborah Brown, a retired Civil Service employee, made important linkages across Norfolk, connecting with area food banks and the faith-based liaison with the NAACP. Deborah's connections also provided access to COVID-19 vaccine resources distributed through churches. Pastor Veronica Thomas was also a passionate driver to provide food for the disadvantaged of Norfolk. Every week she drove to the different communities and delivered food to the hungry. Collectively the team was helping to coordinate distributing eighteen thousand pounds of food monthly across the 757 and ministering to the practical needs of the city's homeless population.

Helping Children Flourish in Education

The 757 and MDVC community developed three primary initiatives educationally. Each of these efforts have received concentrated prayer within city gatherings and on the Saturday Zoom meetings. They pray for God to raise up the next generation's leadership for the church and civic society.

Initiative #1: Increasing Fourth-Grade Literacy Rates

The first initiative focuses on increasing fourth-grade literacy rates, using a Williamsburg school adoption model. Under the leadership of Brandon Randall, this initiative's ten-year vision of the youth engagement design team is to see 100 percent of fourth graders reading at grade level in the seven schools that have been adopted. Brandon is deeply committed to this vision.

In 2021, Williamsburg Community Chapel and New Zion Baptist Church adopted the first two schools as the first initiative. A first step in the strategy, led by Claire Jacobs with support from Leslie Williams and Rebecca Knowles, was to affirm and pray for the teachers. The team adopted seventy-one school staff. Their mission: to write them encouraging notes, pray for them, and provide seventy-five flower arrangements, which Leslie Williams created, that represent the teacher's school colors. They also provided healthy snacks for children who could not afford their own. The design team also hosted a barbeque for the teachers at the end of the school year.

Brandon Randall, executive director at Hospice House and Support Care of Williamsburg, partnered with an after-school book club at Laurel Lane Elementary, one of the adopted schools, with the emphasis on increasing reading skills and comprehension to reach grade level reading by the fourth grade.

The principal at James Blair Middle School, the initial adopted school, said the greatest need was for churches to love these schools and encourage the school staff. The principal has been incredibly supportive of the team prayer walking the campus on Sundays. In the 2021–2022 school year, the plan is to link volunteers with students for tutoring purposes.

Initiative #2: Preparing Students for College

The second initiative is assisting minority young people to prepare for college. Led by Willie Lee, a former Bank of America information technologist and founder of EZ, this initiative is entitled "Going2COLLEGEisEZ." The vision is to help hundreds of minority high-school students be prepared educationally to get accepted into college and to access scholarships to afford college. Willie uses an ACT/SAT prep strategy with a full day of preparation managed by trained facilitators.

He also organizes two bus trips a year of fifty students each to look at two colleges, usually including Howard University, the queen of the Historic Black College and University system. On the ride to the first campus, students watch training videos on preparing for college. At one Maryland campus, qualified students received scholarships on site. In addition, Deborah Brown has also accessed college scholarships through her NAACP connections.

Ron Atkinson, who leads YES USA Campus Thrust, has collaborated with Willie to combine his program with assemblies on high-school campuses. As Atkinson says, "If you can win a campus, you can win a community. If you can win a community, you can win a city. If you can win a city, you can win a country. If you can win a country, you can win 195 nations."

At Taylor High School, Ron was able to influence a principal to host a YES/Dream Assembly on character formation and career options. In addition to casting vision for the educational opportunity, Ron invited students to meet with him if they needed prayer. The work of these two men has been a beautiful marriage of meeting the spiritual and academic needs of young people in the region.

Initiative #3: Engaging At-Risk Young People

A third initiative is to engage at-risk young people in Norfolk. Joe McDaniels, pastor at The Bridge at Park Place, leads an effort in high-risk neighborhoods, running summer programs for grade-school to high-school children. His passion comes from hearing gunshots in his neighborhood almost every night. As a military veteran, he admits many times he has felt his neighborhood is less safe than when he was in military conflict. He led one outreach program on a park basketball court sixteen days after a thirteen-year-old shot and killed a fifteen-year-old at point-blank range at Pollard Street playground. Photos of the fifteen-year-old, a high-school freshman, were posted on the fence near the basketball hoops. This was the ninth shooting death of teens by teens in Norfolk in 2020. It was extraordinary to see Joe's leadership firsthand in October 2020.

Given the enormous educational, economic, and environmental safety issues in the region, the team is also looking at the long-term realities of education and underperforming schools. The discussion is a complex conversation on teacher retention, teacher salaries, unequal availability of funding for schools based on property tax allocations, and how churches can bring effective muscularity to the conversation.

Tackling Homelessness

Another consequence of the COVID-19 pandemic was a spike in homelessness. In Norfolk, city officials created NEST—Norfolk Emergency Shelter Team. The model was to rotate every week with participating churches who could provide housing for the week to several homeless persons. Because of the strict shutdown and "stay-in" government policy, however, almost all of the churches were unable to provide volunteers—except for First Presbyterian Church, one of the 757 members and part of the MDVC community.

Under the leadership of Pastor Jim Wood and Eric Thompson, First Presbyterian volunteered to provide housing the entire October-to-March time frame.

"One of the beauties of the MDVC community is that we were able to support the homeless effort by moving product up and down the 757 peninsula," Eric said. "This included bicycles, Chromebooks for those without computers, and foodstuffs."

Addressing affordable housing is a large and complex topic. One of the 757's working groups is a housing design team that is studying the multiple factors behind the lack of affordable housing. The goal is to think through the challenge in policy form as well as from an immediate strategic perspective.

Managing Business Incubation

In addition to his other work, Eric, along with Khary Bridgewater (see chapter 12), want to encourage and motivate influential Christians to begin investing in minority owned businesses. To that end, they are inviting professional athletes into a conversation about stimulating Black-owned businesses. The vision is to challenge professional athletes to invest in the cities where they play or have played professionally to create job incubation. They see athletes as ambassadors for the vision—to educate other athletes on the strategic nature of capital, and to place athletes into positions of management, using their skill sets to run businesses.

Eric also connected Khary with Jim Franklin, who runs incubator programs focused on minorities. Khary is working to raise hundreds of millions of dollars of capital to assist in acquiring Black-owned businesses to increase employment in fifty cities nationally.

Addressing Spiritual Poverty

What weds all these leaders and churches together is a common spirituality. This spirituality is rooted in the truth of the Bible as a foundation for our lives. And yet, these communities suffer from spiritual poverty. One way they address that is by partnering with the Gideon Movement, which puts Bibles into the hands of people in every imaginable way—on school campuses, in hotels, and in the marketplace. The Williamsburg core group grew out of the Gideon relationship between Clif Brigham, Andy Cronan, and Charlie Williams.

In addition, the 757 wants to broaden addressing spiritual poverty, not only in their region, but throughout the world. During one Saturday Zoom meeting, I introduced the illumiNations twelve-verse challenge. The idea is simple: as a community, memorize twelve verses over the course of a year (such as Romans 12:1–12) and individually resource, through fundraising, the translation of twelve verses at $35 per verse. The challenge is led by an alliance of ten Bible translation agencies with a vision to have the Bible in every one of the remaining 3,800 languages for the 1 billion people without any Scripture. The greatest number of Bibleless peoples are in Africa. The global project, called illumiNations, has a goal to finish every translation by 2033 on the two-thousandth anniversary of Jesus' ascension and they set up a fundraising site (https://www.12vc .com/757beginning).

During that Zoom meeting, I showed the video of the Kimyal people in Indonesia receiving the New Testament for the first time. The sheer sense of joy and emotion was palpable. The video wrecked several 757 members who realized that there were still a billion people without the Bible in their own language.

Led by Don Freeman, pastor of Vineyard Church of the Peninsula, Charlie Williams, Ron Atkinson, and Deborah Brown in turn led design teams for the project. These teams made decisions regarding marketing, project selection, and Scripture memorization.

MDVC/the 757 have a vision to raise $420,000 with one thousand people adopting the twelve-verse challenge and providing

$35 per month for twelve months. Those resources will fund a New Testament, and the books of Genesis, Psalms, and Jonah in an African language. They will resource a language from Africa that was impacted by the slave trade, and the funds will go to a translation agency who will resource the translators and their technical needs.

Awareness to Transformation

When movement takes place, a sense of acceleration and multiplication also takes place. This grows out of the engagement of leaders involved in the movement. Within two years, at least fifteen new initiatives have been birthed or accelerated, involving thousands of people who will become tens of thousands.

Here are just a few ways people have been become aware and how they have responded.

This engagement helped me continue my mother's legacy in her local ministry. The 757 group has inspired me to start a nonprofit that supports important efforts, including food security and providing college scholarships. —Deborah Brown

It is the excitement of seeing things happen as believers work together as churches, nonprofits, and business leaders. I have never seen anything like this in decades of pastoral ministry. —Don Freeman

We must form relationships across barriers to unite with individuals toward the transformation of communities. We get to demonstrate what heaven looks like. This is an army of God's soldiers who have aligned their passions. —Leslie and Charlie Williams

I came as a new learner, praying and lamenting the brokenness between our cultures. I've been impacted by the prayers of tenacity of African-American brothers and sisters. —Faith Olson

I have loved the authenticity of the relationships. I have also loved the idea that we are resourcing each other to scale our collective impact. —Ron Atkinson

Through the interactions and reading, I have just begun to comprehend the level of heartache in the African-American community. I have seen God pull us together into his vision from Isaiah 58 to satisfy the desires of the afflicted. —Andy Cronan

I have been so moved by the prayers of African-American friends and their capacity to worship after having experienced immense suffering. I have seen so much passion in the churches-loving-schools initiative. —Claire Jacobs

This experience has had an amazing, powerful difference in my prayer life. My new African-American friends have been gracious and generous toward me in the midst of my own stupidity. —Mike Morse

This has been the greatest and toughest journey I have ever been on as I turn seventy. I am just coming to grips with the centuries of heartache others have experienced. —Clif Brigham

My involvement has greatly expanded my worldview. It has been an awakening to the possible. —Eric Thompson

Only Just the Beginning

In the past two years this MDVC alliance has seen a radical acceleration of relationships, initiatives, and early-stage outcomes. Those initiatives include:

Thursday prayer
Friday prayer
Weekly Zoom calls
B CARE study groups
Community marches
Police partnerships
School adoption
Going-to-college trips
YES campus outreach
Training virtues
Food security expansion
Homeless volunteerism
Housing research initiative
At-risk youth outreach
Twelve-verse challenge

And they are just getting started. The dream is a ten-year vision to see children educated, economic parity achieved, and communities flourishing for all of their citizens.

We serve a big God, so the members have set their sights on big changes for the kingdom through the work they are doing together. They have discovered a powerful lesson in their coming together: the spark of awareness married to opportunities to go deeper in relationships will produce a movement of accelerated impact.

Part Two

OWNERSHIP:
MERCY
REQUIRED

Chapter 8

BEYOND SYMPATHY
TO OWNERSHIP

Claude

In the immediate aftermath of the tragic shooting at Mother Emanuel Church in Charleston, South Carolina, in which nine persons lost their lives, the sympathy of the nation and even the world overflowed. But too soon, the news cycle focused on a different event, and the people whose lives had been forever altered now faded out of the spotlight; for many it was a tragic, but now forgotten, story.

As meaningful as expressions of sympathy are, they do not tend to produce significant and sustainable change. Sympathy sends us cards and brings us food for a week. But sympathy has its limits, and life moves on, leaving little truly changed.

While sympathy is good and important, God calls us to move beyond sympathy to press for something lasting. When something really needs to be done, when people need to be cared for, fought for, we must move beyond sympathy and into ownership. Ownership causes us not simply to look as an observer, but to enter as a participant and agent of change.

Ownership is what caused White men and women along with Jews to travel southward in 1964 to participate in Freedom Summer, a volunteer effort to register as many Black voters as possible in Mississippi.

Ownership is what caused many to converge on Selma, Alabama, in 1965, and march fifty-four miles to the state capital of Montgomery to place pressure on lawmakers to pass the Voting Rights Act.

Ownership is what causes a person to be willing to take risky action. It promotes sacrifice, the giving up of ourselves for the benefit and promotion of another. This is mercy at its best.

Jesus gives us an example of this kind of merciful ownership in His parable of the Good Samaritan:

On one occasion an expert in the law stood up to test Jesus. "Teacher," he asked, "what must I do to inherit eternal life?"

"What is written in the Law?" he replied. "How do you read it?"

He answered, "'Love the Lord your God with all your heart and with all your soul and with all your strength and with all your mind'; and, 'Love your neighbor as yourself.'"

"You have answered correctly," Jesus replied. "Do this and you will live."

But he wanted to justify himself, so he asked Jesus, "And who is my neighbor?"

In reply Jesus said: "A man was going down from Jerusalem to Jericho, when he was attacked by robbers. They stripped him of his clothes, beat him and went away, leaving him half dead. A priest happened to be going down the same road, and when he saw the man, he passed by on the other side. So too, a Levite, when he came to the place and saw him, passed by on the other side. But a Samaritan, as he traveled, came where the man was; and when he saw him, he took pity on him. He went to him and bandaged his wounds, pouring on oil and wine. Then he put the man on his own donkey, brought him to an inn and took care of him. The next day he took out two denarii and gave them to the innkeeper. 'Look after him,' he said, 'and when I return, I will reimburse you for any extra expense you may have.'" (Luke 10:25–35)

Jesus tells this parable within the context of a conversation with a Jewish official concerned about eternal life. The answer is to love the Lord your God and to love your neighbor as yourself. Trying to find the parameters of what Jesus means by loving a neighbor, the official asks about the identity of the neighbor. In response, Jesus tells the parable. In telling it, He doesn't identify the neighbor. He identifies only the one who acts neighborly. He does it in such a way that He demonstrates the difference between sympathy and solidarity, or mercy.

This man, this neighbor, is traveling from Jerusalem to Jericho. He is presumably a Jew. On his way, robbers attack him. They steal his belongings, strip him of his clothes, beat him, and leave him in the street half dead.

A priest comes down the road, sees the man, crosses to the other side of the street, and keeps walking.

A Levite does the same thing.

But then a Samaritan enters the story. By introducing this person as a Samaritan, Jesus invokes the issue of race. Samaritans were people of mixed blood. In fact, the term *Samaritan* was a pejorative. They were frowned upon by the Orthodox Jews as being the lowest of the low. This Samaritan comes to where the beaten man is, sees him, has pity on him, bandages him, puts him on his own donkey, takes him to an inn, sees to his medical care, pays for him to stay there, and ensures his continued care by telling the innkeeper that he will cover any other costs upon his return.

Within this story, Jesus reveals what it means to respond to the moment by going beyond sympathy and into solidarity. All three characters are presented with the same moment—that opportunity to do something to aid the injured man. The first two respond one way—they avoid. Yet their avoidance keeps the moment alive. Had either of them responded differently, there wouldn't have been a moment for the third character. The issue would have been handled. The problem would have been solved. But because of the way they handled the situation, the moment presented itself to the third character.

Unlike the first two, the third person, the Samaritan, took ownership. And in that example, Jesus challenged His listeners—and us—to become the Samaritan.

Ownership Challenges Us to Reaching Beyond "the Limits"

Jesus alerted the lawyer that inheriting eternal life is tied to loving the Lord his God with all his heart, his soul, his strength, his mind, and to loving his neighbor as himself. But that's an uncomfortable proposition. So the official, trying to find the parameters of loving his neighbor, asks about this "neighbor's" identity. Surely there must be a limit, a line, an out that God provides in whom the official should love as he loves himself. There must be some categories of exemption. There *must* be restrictions.

Jesus' response becomes, in essence, the first challenge he issues to the man. He wants him to realize that it isn't how narrowly you can restrict but how broadly you can reach.

Jesus broadens the view by showing a Samaritan who rejects

categories of limitation. He calls us to recognize the essential humanity in all people and see them as subjects for offering compassion and mercy. Jesus challenges the young official and us to be broad in the focus of our compassionate/neighborly concern. The kingdom question is never, *How narrow is my restriction?* It is always, *How broad is my reach?*

God's reach is universal and global: "God so loved *the world*" (John 3:16). Since we are to be like Jesus, our reach must be broad and boundless as well.

Ownership Challenges Us to Get a Close-Up View

The second challenge Jesus issues for ownership is that we must move closer than others are willing to move—close enough to the moment to realize what we can't understand from a distance. The particulars of the story are important. The man was robbed, stripped, beaten, and left half dead. As both the priest and Levite approached, they saw this man from a distance, so they crossed the street—keeping their distance—and continued walking. One of the reasons was that from a distance, the half-dead man looked dead. From a distance, the situation looked terminal. From a distance, it looked like a case for the undertaker and not for them. Their distance caused them to make a judgment upon which they acted. They acted off of a perception from a distance. It's not personal or proximal.

With Jesus not giving us the amount of time that elapsed between the priest and the Levite, it is possible that the Levite watched the priest's actions and just did the same thing. Or, if there was more time between them, the victim could have looked more dead from a distance to the Levite than to the priest. And so neither of them came close to the man. Neither entered the man's neighborhood. Neither checked their distant assumptions with closer examination.

The Samaritan, on the other hand, walked to the man. He did not base his actions on how the man looked from a distance. He moved close, which allowed him to see more clearly and realistically. He realized what he could not understand at a distance. At a distance, he was prone to make certain judgments. But once he drew closer, he saw the man as he was.

God is calling us to move beyond making judgments from a distance and come into knowledge through proximity. We must be willing to enter into the space, the neighborhood, the reality, and see things for what they really are, see people for who they really are, know the issues for what they really are. In mercy, we refuse to accept the distant judgments of others, and instead risk coming close enough to see for ourselves.

By moving close enough, the Samaritan saw that the man who looked dead from a distance was only half dead in reality. When he entered the man's proximity, he was able to correctly and properly identify him. By coming close, he recognized in the man what he knew about himself. While faintly, the man was breathing. Though weak, the man had a pulse. Though wounded and broken, he still had life. He still bore the image of God. He still had meaning, value, and dignity. He still deserved a chance to get better and to be better.

God is calling us into the lives of others and to recognize in others that what is true for us is also true for them. We all have been endowed with a need to be and to belong. We all desire the opportunity to be our best selves. We all desire safety and security for ourselves and for those whom we love. All parents want their children to be educated in safe schools by competent and caring teachers who value them and see them in terms of their potential. All people want to live in safe neighborhoods with neither the fear of crime nor the false assumption of criminality by law enforcement. Every man wants to be respected as a man, and every woman wants equal pay for a day's work.

Move close. Get a close-up view and see what God shows you.

Ownership Challenges Us to Value Life above Excuses

From a distance, the priest and the Levite crossed the street and kept walking, not simply because they feared the man. They crossed to keep distant, out of desire to remain ceremonially clean. Levitical law forbade them from coming into contact with a dead body. Seeing what they believed to be a dead body, their concerns over ceremonial cleanliness overrode their concern for the man.

Not so with the Samaritan. His priority was the man's condition. Concern for the man moved the Samaritan closer. And what he saw revealed a willingness to value the life above what the normal excuses would be.

It is here that question of ownership was raised. Now that he knew, would he own it? The Samaritan revealed something crucial about ownership. We must be willing to value life above what normal excuses may be. The priest and the Levite saw a man who looked dead, so they crossed the street not wanting to become unclean. The law became their reason for not coming closer. Their concern for their status kept them at a distance.

The Samaritan moved closer, not worried about his status. His movement caused him to see that what others thought would have been an issue wasn't an issue at all. His valuing what he saw at a distance moved him closer. He moved beyond the normal excuses.

If we are to experience true ownership and mercy, we must be willing to value life in such a way that we overcome the normal excuses to proximity: *I don't know them. They aren't my people. It's not worth the hassle.*

When you value the person, when you recognize the image of God in the person, you become willing to overcome the normal excuses for being against them.

Ownership Challenges Us to Be Impacted by the Condition of Others

Up close to the man, the Samaritan didn't know where the robbers were. They could have been hiding in a bush. They could have been around the corner, or just down the street. Stopping was risky. Yet the Samaritan took the risk of looking at the man, of really seeing him, of becoming aware. He saw that the man, while half dead, was also half alive. In seeing the man, he took pity on him. He had compassion. He felt for him. He experienced empathy.

Ownership requires a willingness to be impacted by the condition of others. Just as the Samaritan felt for the person he saw, we are called to feel for the people we see. We are called to see them and to feel them. It is the challenge to see and feel their hopes, their fears, their joys, their hurts, their pain, their frustrations, their brokenness.

Seeing what he saw, feeling what he felt, and knowing what he knew, he determined to do something to change the moment, the situation. He couldn't leave the man in his current condition. The moment called for him to respond. So he bent down. He got on the man's level. He got dust on his clothes and dirt under his nails. He got blood on his clothes as he bandaged the man and lifted him onto his own donkey.

Ownership fueled by mercy occurs when we slow down to become aware of another's experience and condition, such that we see them for who they really are and grasp the severity of their condition. We become open to such a degree that we are personally impacted. Ownership fueled by mercy is the willingness to be personally impacted, to become vulnerable to the point of being shaken into action. We know that we cannot allow things to remain as they are—we must do something. We must become personally involved.

The Samaritan's ownership included taking on the risk of identifying with the other person and by making sacrifices and getting on a different level—that person's level—expecting nothing in return.

Henry Dunant understood the power of ownership. Born in 1828 to wealthy parents in Geneva, Switzerland, Henry grew up in a home of devout Christians who stressed the importance of social work. When he turned eighteen years old, Henry joined the Geneva Society for Alms Giving. One year later, he and his friends founded the "Thursday Association," which met to study the Bible and help the poor. Later, he founded the Geneva chapter of the YMCA.

One evening, in 1859, while traveling to meet with Emperor Napoleon III, Dunant came across the aftermath of a bloody battle in Solferino, Italy. Some forty thousand men—wounded, dying, and dead lay across the field. Moved with compassion, he put his personal agenda aside and helped the doctors care for the needs of the people. The experience had such an effect upon him that he wrote about it, describing the battle, the costs, the brutality of war, and of the need for a neutral organization to provide care to wounded soldiers. This resulted in the Geneva Convention of 1864, with twenty-two nations signing accords acknowledging the neutrality of medical personnel in time of conflict. They chose a red cross on a white field for their banner and symbol. This gave birth to the Red Cross.[1]

If we are to be the church God is calling us to be, we must embrace ownership and allow ourselves to become impacted by the condition of others.

Ownership Challenges Us to Devote a Long-Term Commitment

Ownership always comes with a cost. The cost is often giving up convenience and schedules and privilege. It is being willing to suffer discomfort on behalf of another. It is to bend toward another. It's to get dirty with another. It's to experience delay in order to help another. And it is doing it all while expecting nothing in return.

The Samaritan gave up the privilege of riding on his donkey. By putting the wounded man on the donkey, the Samaritan had to walk. He adjusted his schedule. He went out of his way to make sure the man was taken care of.

There was nothing about the man that would cause the Samaritan to think he'd receive anything in return for his help. His ownership was not about career expansion, networking, or resume improvement. He had no expectation of receiving quid pro quo or an IOU. He was simply working to improve a situation without looking for or expecting anything in return. His value of the man made him desire to make the man's situation better.

The calculus of your actions is not what you'll get from it. It's what you give to it. It's not how it benefits you. It's how you benefit it. It's simply determining that there is something you can do to make it better. Your listening made it better. Your understanding made it better. Your stopping made it better. Your speaking made it better. Your counseling made it better.

The Samaritan did what he could to make it better. Bandaging the man's wounds and taking him to the inn would have been enough. It was more than most would do. However, the Samaritan took it another step. He made provision for the man's long-term care. He gave the innkeeper two days' wages and told him to look after the man, and that when he returned, he would reimburse the innkeeper for any extra expense. He wasn't satisfied with the short-term quick fix. He invested in the long-term, in seeing the outcome through.

Authentic care includes a commitment to the long-term. It desires lasting change. It wants things to be well not just today, not just tomorrow, but also next week, next month, and next year. It moves you to raise long-term questions and to provide long-term solutions. It's not just about helping somebody out of a situation. It's about addressing the factors that put them into the situation, giving them a better option than the situation, shutting down the forces that created the situation in the first place.

The Samaritan committed himself to the long-term.

We Show Mercy by Loving Our Neighbor

When Jesus finished telling the parable, He asked the official, "Which of these three do you think was a neighbor to the man who fell into the hands of robbers?" (Luke 10:36).

The official answered the one who had mercy, the one who showed solidarity. Jesus then told the official, "Go and do likewise" (v. 37).

Jesus says the same to us. Go and do likewise. Go and be the neighbor. Go further and see people for who they really are. Follow God's requirement and care and overcome your normal excuses for being against them. Go and be impacted by their condition, such that you are willing to take ownership. Go and do likewise.

But we aren't just being like the Samaritan. We're being like Jesus. He demonstrated answering those challenges. He was not a cosmic spectator and eternal observer. He came into our neighborhood and saw us for who we really are. He was touched with the feeling of our infirmities, and tempted of all that tempts us. Seeing us in our helpless estate, dead in sins, He took ownership for our reconciliation. With there being nothing we could give in return that would add to who He is, Jesus gave it all up on our behalf.

In His mercy, He sought ownership with us. How can we not do the same for others?

Claude's family: (front row from left) Mother Dr. Otrie Hickerson-Smith
and Father Dr. Robert Smith; (back row from left) Claude, Brother Robert
Smith, Jr., Sister Donna Smith, and Aunt Gladys Smith

Claude and Mac Everett, co-chair of the Community
Building Initiative, Charlotte, North Carolina

Claude speaking at The Park Church, Charlotte

Claude with daughters (from left)
Camryn and Carsyn, and wife,
Kim (far right)

Mac and his siblings: (from left) Erin, Michele,
Mac (age 4), Rick, and Renee

Mac and Marya (center) and their extended family from five nations

Eric Thompson, Movement ForORF director and Mary Bibbs of Bibbs Firm, LLC, working at the food distribution event in Norfolk, Virginia, in 2020. Photo courtesy of Ronald J Atkinson, www.urbanstockhouse.net.

Jack Alexander (left) and the One Race team, including Josh Clemons, executive director (far right)

Mac and Claude with leaders Stephen Mbogo of African Enterprise (second from right) and Nana Yaw of Lausanne (far right) at Movement Day Africa in Nairobi, 2018

City Collective organized a city-wide, church unity event in downtown Norfolk, 2020.
The march included 5,000 participants.
Photo courtesy of Joanna Atkinson, www.urbanstockhouse.net.

Nigel Legin Anderson (left) and Kevin Tremper, organizers of City
Collective's 5,000 celebration march, Norfolk, Virginia.
Photo courtesy of Ronald J Atkinson, www.urbanstockhouse.net.

Anglo and African-American pastors praying for a next generation leader; Dale Evrist (left), Jymme Foot, Robbie Owen; City Advance, October 2012, New York City

Khary Bridgewater, founder and CEO of Norstell Capital and the architect of Inspire Equity

Peter Watt of 3C Church (left) partnering with Robert Ntuli to address xenophobia in Durban, South Africa

Mac speaking at Movement Day Global Cities in 2016

Claude speaking at Movement Day Global Cities in 2016

Chapter 9

ONE RACE: JACK ALEXANDER'S JOURNEY INTO MERCY

Mac

Jack Alexander has less than five memories of his father. His father, a successful businessman, traveled extensively for his job and was rarely home long enough to spend any time with Jack or his two older sisters.

When Jack was nine years old, his father died. Though his dad had been ill for a year, no one had ever bothered to tell Jack. The family never discussed it.

Even at that young age, though Jack had become used to his father being gone all the time, the news of his dad's death still shocked him. It shocked everyone. Jack's mom fully expected her husband to be healed. And when he wasn't, fear and despair took over their home.

To make matters worse, their minister told the family that their father's death frustrated God.

"Frustrated God?" Jack says. "If there is an atheist switch, mine turned on in that moment."

Life turned very quickly for the Alexander family. His mother did her best to care for them and to keep their family financially afloat—even eventually marrying a man she did not love to help her family survive. But the great loss threw Jack into survival living with no spiritual or emotional foundation.

The one thing his mother was most adamant about was her children's education, so she took the scant insurance money she received after her husband's death to send Jack and his siblings to a prep school and then college.

As soon as Jack graduated from high school, he left his hometown of West Hartford, Connecticut, and headed to Duke University. After graduation, he took a job with the Arthur Andersen accounting firm in Atlanta. For the next four years, though he worked hard and struggled to do well, the pain he carried from his childhood lingered. He had no father figure and no spiritual foundation. He needed a change. So when an opportunity arose to transfer to Melbourne, Australia, in 1977, with his company, he jumped at the chance. He was twenty-six.

Not long after he arrived, he realized he was alone in a new way. He knew no one—and had 0 percent chance of running into anyone from "back home." Isolation and loneliness became his companions and made him wonder about the meaning and purpose in life.

"I didn't want to work until seventy or eighty years of age, then get put in a hole in the ground," Jack says.

Those doubts and ponderings began to soften his heart and prepare him to be open to hearing about God in a new way. In the coming weeks, he met Lynn through mutual friends in Melbourne. Lynn was a passionate and enthusiastic follower of Jesus who loved the church. "I was from Connecticut, where no one I knew was ever excited about God, and certainly not a church," Jack says.

Not long after, he met Alan who had a healing and deliverance ministry. Alan was so engaging and different from Christians he had met before that he wanted to know more about God. Alan invited him to participate in his weekly healing and deliverance sessions at his house. And Alan put Jack to work as his "catcher"— catching people as they fainted during the deliverance session.

"Alan often told me, 'God can do anything, and He can do anything through you.'"

Finally, Jack met a pastor named Jim, whose preaching of the gospel opened Jack's heart. Jim did an altar call for people to come forward to receive Christ as Savior and Lord. He then added, "Don't come forward unless you are willing to give Jesus all you are and all you have."

Jack was up for the challenge and gave his heart and life to God. For the remainder of his time "down under," he spent time with these three believers, allowing them to mentor him.

When his contract was up and he was set to return to the United States, he met once more with Jim.

"I want to pray over you before you leave," Jim told him and encouraged him to get on his knees.

Jack did so, and Jim prayed John 17 over him—the prayer in which Jesus desired for the church to be one in unity.

At the end of the prayer, Jim looked Jack directly in the eyes and said, "Go back to America and unite God's church."

"Huh?" Jack was a young accountant traveling back to Atlanta with many unknowns. And he was poor, having given his $1,000 savings to their church. "But I did have a new Father, a new Savior, and the Spirit of God to guide me, comfort me, and to lead me into truth," Jack says.

Jack was amazed by the lengths God would go to reach him.

And as he returned to America, his heart and eyes were wide open to receive what mission God had for him.

Discipled in Atlanta

Back in Atlanta, Jack set out to find a church home and landed at Perimeter Church. There he connected with the church's pastor, Randy Pope, as well as Bob Lupton, founder and president of Focused Community Strategies and author of *Theirs Is the Kingdom: The Gospel in Urban America.*

Randy taught Jack about worship, evangelism, discipleship, and a love for Scripture. And Bob taught him about neighboring and the kingdom of God. Bob had moved into one of Atlanta's high-crime districts to bring the gospel and its impact to his community. Though Jack had never encountered the kinds of challenges Bob's neighborhood presented, Jack opened himself to the possibility that this space might be exactly where God had placed him. Under Randy and Bob's influence, Jack began to see the needs of Atlanta through a different lens.

As Jack continued to grow in his faith, he read *The Unshakable Kingdom and the Unchanging Person* by E. Stanley Jones. In it Jones talks about organizing our whole lives around the kingdom of God—humility, servanthood, small things, weaknesses, neighboring, and mercy.

Jack began to think more about what that meant in his life: The vertical gospel of Christ rescuing us when we were dead in our sins; the glorious truth that we, through Christ, can be born again, because He laid down His life for us; that just as He laid down His life, we in turn love our brothers and sisters by our willingness to lay down our lives for them. This becomes the horizontal gospel—loving our neighbors.

It was under Bob's tutelage that Jack began to grapple with Matthew 25 and a description of Jesus' "six friends"—the hungry, thirsty, homeless, impoverished, sick, and imprisoned. Jack began to reflect on the vertical gospel, which focuses on our relationship with God, and the horizontal gospel, which focuses on our neighbor. Then he looked more closely at the Ten Commandments in the Old Testament and noted that six of the ten focused on our relationship with our neighbor: honoring our parents, not murdering, not committing adultery, not stealing, not giving false testimony, not coveting.

Finally, from Matthew 5, Jack reflected on Jesus' command to leave our gift at the altar to be reconciled one with another. Jesus' focus on horizontal relationships was more important than being financially generous as a value. Jack realized that forgiveness and reconciliation are the currency that keep a spiritual community together, and that helped him better understand an integrated view of God and neighbor.

"The polarization we face in our communities and world can be addressed by embracing the vertical gospel enthusiastically and letting God's grace and mercy through us liberally lap over into the lives of our neighbors in the horizontal gospel, including the vulnerable and our enemies," Jack said.

Now he knew the mission God was calling him to, and he understood the Australian pastor's prayer over him. And it started with his own life history. God had shown him mercy throughout his life, and Jack wanted to show others that kind of loving mercy as well. And where best to start? Going to children who were also without fathers.

From his time with Bob, he knew that high-crime communities had overwhelming numbers of fatherless children. That's where he wanted to start. "I discovered from the moment of my father's death that pain and passion are first cousins," Jack says. "We often have passion in the area where we have been hurt the most. Living in a single-parent home is where fear dominates and marks us. When I see the extent of fatherlessness in the African-American community, it breaks my heart." It was time to do something about it.

A Global Professional Platform

For the next forty years, Jack leveraged his professional success to become a champion for the poor. In 1999, Ernst and Young named him National Entrepreneur of the Year for Principle-Centered Leadership. He was also a six-time award winner of *Business Travel News*' top twenty-five most influential executives. Jack cofounded BCD Travel and TRX, which grew to six thousand employees and $350 million in revenue. And he used his platform to speak, write, and advocate for the poor and fatherless.

When he learned that one of his sons had three members of his high-school golf team who had lost their dads to suicide, Jack immediately reached out. Their family developed a relationship with these young men, whom he mentored for the next eighteen years. Jack and his wife, Lisa, even funded them to attend college. They became so intimately involved in the young men's lives that they sat at the head table at each of their weddings.

One of the most profound mentoring relationships Jack took on was cross-culturally with Barron McCoy, a young African American. Their friendship has lasted more than thirty-seven years. It all started when Barron was thirteen years old. His mother struggled as a single parent to raise him and his sister. Jack knew that experience intimately and determined that Barron wouldn't grow up without a solid and stable father figure in his life, as Jack had. Jack took him under his wing, giving him his first job and advocating for him when he was in trouble. Though Jack had grown up without a father, he was able to show mercy to others in the same situation and used that mercy to show up as a dad in their lives.

And God continued to expand his mission. He saw the impact in India of farmers who committed suicide after crop failure, leaving their wives and children destitute. So he invested in Friends of the Poor, a group that supported 3,000 widows of former farmers and saw 1,800 of these widows become followers of Jesus.

Living as the Good Samaritan

In 2017, Jack found himself sitting in the congregation of Venture Christian Church and listening to a guest speaker preach a message based on the life of the Good Samaritan. That speaker was Claude.[1] As he listened, the message resonated with what he had recently been thinking and writing about. Jack was, in fact, writing *The God Impulse: The Power of Mercy in an Unmerciful World*. Hearing Claude was in many ways a culmination of Jack's own journey through fatherlessness, salvation, discipleship, career development, and racial engagement.

What really struck him was when Claude said, "The racial divide is not our fault, but it is our problem." That statement validated Jack's engagement with the racial divide in his own city of Atlanta.

Even though Jack had been active in building cross-cultural friendships and mentoring the fatherless, it was Claude's teaching that helped him synthesize what he needed to know from an historical perspective. Though Jack was familiar with the Good Samaritan parable, the way Claude shared it changed something within him. It became the paradigm that brought all his life themes together.

Later that day and into the following days and weeks, Claude's message stayed with Jack. As a believer, his church had helped teach him to see and think. The story of the Good Samaritan taught him how to see and *feel*. He recognized that too many people felt unloved by the church. "We need to go to Samaria—the place of racial and ethnic tension," Jack says. "Second Corinthians

8:9 says that Jesus made Himself poor to make us rich. Christians have to ask ourselves two questions, 'How am I making myself poor?' and 'Which of my neighbors am I making rich?'"

These were questions he began to ask himself. "My heart was just heavy. . . . I was surprised how ignorant I was about the history [of racism in America]. It was like being in a closet when the lights are off and someone turns on the light. It set me on fire."[2]

Since hearing that life-changing message, Jack has reflected on the Good Samaritan and describes it as the "pattern of love." The pattern begins with "seeing" the needs around us, as the Good Samaritan saw. It is important to be observant and aware.

The next part of the pattern is to feel mercy, which compels us to "go." Going involves taking the initiative to approach people in pain. It is about leaving our comfort zone to make a difference.

The third piece of the pattern is to "do." The Good Samaritan brought the injured traveler to the inn and paid for his care. He made the sacrifice of time, effort, and investment. It did not matter to the Good Samaritan that the person was a stranger and from a different ethnic/religious background. It mattered only that the person needed help.

The final part of the pattern is to "endure." The Good Samaritan promised to return and to check on the victim. He promised to pay any unmet expenses.

The following year, in 2018, Jack got connected to the One Race Atlanta movement, which is a coalition of Christian leaders from diverse racial backgrounds. One Race convenes leaders to listen, learn, and engage on the themes of reconciliation and revival. The One Race Atlanta is dedicated to teaching its citizens to love, regardless of color, class, and culture. And its pillars are personal and cultural transformation through unity, and passionate love for God and one another.

On August 28, 2018—the fifty-fifth anniversary of Martin Luther King Jr.'s "I Have a Dream" speech—One Race convened twenty-five thousand people to gather and pray. Jack was so moved by the experience that he continued his involvement, even taking on the role as their board chair.

In 2019, Jack spoke at a men's retreat at Saint James Church, where he extended an apology on behalf of his ancestors for the history of slavery in the United States. In response, many African-American men got in line to meet him. "I was the first person whom many of those in attendance had heard express those sentiments," he says. "There was a line of 150 African Americans who gathered to greet me after my presentation."

As a result of his involvement in the One Race Movement, Jack has initiated several efforts to impact Atlanta, including the Leadership 400 Fund, which has a vision to benefit African-American leaders to empower the next generation toward a trajectory of professional success. The Leadership 400 Fund gave funding to Peace Prep, which provided education for young African Americans.

Another initiative is the Geronimo Fund, which Jack started in 2003 and named after the famed Apache chief. Geronimo was known for going into the hardest places to fight the battle. Beyond his Atlanta-based philanthropy, Jack has assisted with Native Americans going to college through the fund. He has also used the fund to partner with the International Justice Mission in addressing those in slavery globally. They raised millions of dollars in just the first two years for mercy and justice projects in twenty-six countries.

Becoming a Spiritual Father

Over the arc of his life, Jack discovered a depth and dimension of God's Fatherhood in his own life. He encountered God's provisional care through his Melbourne church experience. The pain of his own fatherlessness gave him empathy toward the fatherlessness on a massive scale in the African-American community. Through his openness to be mentored by the likes of Bob Lupton and Claude, he received the grace and generosity of spirit to understand his leadership role in the context of the American church experience.

Now at the age of seventy, the call to mercy remains an enormous part of Jack's legacy. He has invested both locally and globally toward those who have suffered injustices. And he continues to be determined not to waste any of the mercy he has received. Jack has demonstrated the mercy of a father through his investment in other fatherless young men by embracing the call to mercy in a cross-cultural movement, and to invest practically into the unmet needs of the multitudes locally and globally.

Part Three

AGENCY: JUSTICE REQUIRED

Chapter 10

EXERCISING AGENCY

Claude

In May 2020, an interfaith group of clergy began preparing a Charlotte community prayer vigil to acknowledge the one-hundred-thousand COVID-19-death mark. We were all taken aback by the enormity of loss that had taken place and sought to provide a means of lament, resolve, and hope. We set the date for the service for May 29. Four days before our service, on May 25, with us focusing on final preparations, George Floyd was killed in Minneapolis after Police Officer Derek Chauvin knelt on his neck and back for more than nine minutes.

Immediately, the conversation turned to the question, How should we respond? Should we not hold the vigil? Should we change the focus of the vigil? Should we merge the two and focus on both the COVID deaths and George Floyd's? How should and would we use the platform we had?

This was the first of many such conversations in which we, along with people throughout the country, asked the same questions: "How can and should we respond? What should we do to affect change?" These are the questions of agency.

Those who would seek to make a difference must heed the call to own where we have been, where we are, and where we hope to go—then use that ownership to work toward making things right and just in positive and redemptive ways. Ownership and acting on it go hand in hand. That action is what we call agency. Social psychologist Albert Bandura describes agency as being

> the human capability to influence one's functioning and the course of events by one's actions. There are four functions through which human agency is exercised. One such function is intentionality. People form intentions that include action plans and strategies for realizing them. The second function involves temporal extension of agency through forethought. People set themselves goals and foresee likely outcomes of prospective actions to guide and motivate their efforts anticipatorily. The third agentic function is self-reactiveness. Agents are not only planners and forethinkers. They are also self-regulators. The fourth agentic function is self-reflectiveness. People are not only agents, they are self-examiners of their own functioning. Through functional self-awareness, they reflect on their personal efficacy, the soundness of their thoughts and actions, the meaning of their pursuits, and make corrective adjustments if necessary.[1]

While everyone possesses agency, not everyone fully exercises the agency that they possess. In the course of my work as a pastor, along with my work with the Community Building Initiative and with Christian organizations and city movements seeking to understand and address matters of racism, I have come to see that we can use our agency in five types or categories—and they are all ways we can "do justly," as God requires of us in Micah 6:8:

- Personal agency arises out of who you are as an individual—your talents, gifts, anointing, experience, exposure, interests, etc. This is agency in just you being who you are. It is the capacity to influence people and circumstances from the power of who you are as a person. It is bringing the sum total of your talent, gifting, anointing, experiences, and exposure to a given conversation, interaction, or engagement. It is also the example that you set before people.
- Practical agency is how you bring who you are to bear and influence what you can control. This is whom you choose to be in any given moment; what you choose to do; where you choose to go; how you choose to act; where, when, and how you choose to insert and assert yourself in a given situation.
- Positional agency is the capacity that you possess through the various roles and positions you inhabit. There is agency I possess as a man, as a son, as a husband, as a father, as a brother, as a preacher, as a pastor, as a board member, etc. Positional agency is using the position you hold to amplify and extend an issue of concern.
- Political agency is the capacity to influence and alter through advocacy and voting. You count. You matter. Through the census, you help decide how many representatives we have, how districts are drawn, how funds are disbursed to the state, where funds go to needy programs. Your voice matters when you show up at council, commission, school board, and public hearing meetings. You count when you register and vote on ballot initiatives and candidates.
- Pecuniary agency is economic in nature. It is the capacity to influence by how you spend, when you spend, where you spend, with whom you bank and invest.

At its very core, agency is God-ordained. The capacity to choose, to determine, to reflect, to adjust, to create, to transform, are part of the *imago Dei*. It's conferred upon us as those who are created after His image and likeness. It is what distinguishes us from the rest of creation. It has as its purpose the performance of the good that God foreordained. As Paul wrote in Ephesians 2:10, "We are God's masterpiece. He has created us anew in Christ Jesus, so we can do the good things he planned for us long ago" (NLT).

The agency that we possess is for the good that God has planned.

We are in a season where God is calling us to recognize and exercise the agency we have for the good that He has planned. We cannot sit back and look for others to exercise their agency. We can't delegate the agentic to others. Each of us must hear and heed God's call to agency.

Esther Was Called On to Use Her Agency

The story of Esther provides an example of hearing and heeding God's call to agency. Esther's family was among those Jews taken into captivity by Nebuchadnezzar of Babylon. They remained in Babylon when the Persians took over the area. Now Esther's only remaining family was an uncle named Mordecai. When she vied for the position of queen, he advised her to keep her Jewish identity a secret.

In the meantime, Xerxes, king of Persia, elevated Haman above all of the Persian princes. All the servants of the king, with the exception of Mordecai, paid homage to Haman. Haman took offense at Mordecai's failure to bow to him. Rather than kill him, Haman sought to destroy all of Mordecai's people.

Shortly after Xerxes coronated Esther, Haman set the evil plot in motion. He informed Xerxes that the Jews weren't keeping his laws and were a threat to the advancement of his kingdom.

Therefore, the king should decree that they be destroyed and pay those who would kill them. Xerxes agreed and had the decree written. The time for execution was to be the thirteenth day of the twelfth month. All Jews, both young and old, little children and women, were to be killed.

When Mordecai learned of the edict, he was understandably devastated. Esther became aware of his distress, and she sent a messenger to find out the reason. Mordecai informed the messenger of the plot to destroy the people, sent him back with the text of the edict, and urged Esther to go before the king to seek mercy on behalf of her people.

Esther responded by saying that it would be out of order for her to do so, because the king had not called for her to appear before him.

Mordecai responded:

Do not think that because you are in the king's house you alone of all the Jews will escape. For if you remain silent at this time, relief and deliverance for the Jews will arise from another place, but you and your father's family will perish. And who knows but that you have come to your royal position for such a time as this? (Esther 4:13–14)

Agency Comes with an Awakening to Our Assignment

Mordecai sought to awaken Esther to the agency that she could and should exercise as queen. When he reminded her of the positional agency she held as queen, Esther refused, based upon her sense of timing. It would not be the best move for her to make. It could work against her in a major way. Those with advancement in mind, not to mention mere survival, would not even think of doing such a thing.

Then Mordecai highlighted the connection between her

and her people. In so doing, the whole notion of responsibility enlarged. She was not simply responsible for herself. She was responsible for her people. The well-being of her people was connected to how she operated in the position where God placed her. She was encouraged to think of those whose lives were connected to her and whose futures were dependent upon her.

Mordecai went further to assert that the reason she was placed as queen was to intercede on behalf of the people. If this was true, then it meant that God knew of the need before the need existed. God placed her before the problem, knowing that the problem would come. If this was true, then her full purpose could not be realized until the problem came. God positioned her in order to be the solution to the problem. God saw it in advance and placed her in the role of queen to handle it when it arose. This would require that she become aware, take ownership, and use her agency to do something about it. She could not pass it off to anyone else, because no one else had been placed by God in the position she occupied to be the solution God had foreordained.

Agency arises from knowing that with awareness comes an assignment that can't be delegated. What is brought to you demands something from you. Because you see it, sense it, feel it, and understand it, you are personally called to it. This isn't about what someone else saw, heard, felt, understood, or knew. If it was for others, they would have seen it, heard it, felt it, understood it, or known it. But since you've seen it, heard it, felt it, understood it, and known it, it's for you to do something in response. It calls for the exercise of your agency. It calls for the lifting of your voice. It calls for the giving of your time, your talent, your treasure. Your awareness means your assignment.

In response to Robert Putnam's 2000 Social Capital Community Benchmark survey, which showed that Charlotte ranked thirty-nine out of forty cities with regard to interracial trust, leaders of institutions were challenged to look at how, within the grid of their missions, they could exercise agency in addressing the issue. Among those who took their awareness as their assignment were Dr. Maria Hanlin, the executive director of Mecklenburg Ministries, and Judge Shirley Fulton, the first African American to serve as the senior resident Superior Court Judge in Mecklenburg County.

Dr. Hanlin first instituted Friday Friends, where clergy of different racial backgrounds met on Fridays for lunch to develop personal relationships and discuss issues of race. She then followed it with the course, "Souls of White Folks," which engaged White clergy to reflect upon the nature and reality of "White privilege." White clergy leaders spent several months reflecting upon personal and collective histories. They followed that up by hearing the personal stories of people of color.

Judge Fulton responded by instituting a study within the 26th Judicial District of North Carolina to determine the presence and level of disparate treatment in the courts based on race, gender, ethnicity, or religion. Studying case analysis of closed cases, as well as exit interviews of persons involved in drug administrative court and district traffic court, neither the cases analyzed nor the participants interviewed showed bias or disparate treatment. Under her leadership in a program called Leadership in a Diverse Community, district and superior court judges were educated on race issues related to justice.[2]

A more recent example of awareness translating into ownership is that of Shirley V. Hoogstra, the president of the Council for Christian Colleges & Universities. I met Shirley during a Civilitas conversation on race in 2016. Afterward, she asked me to join the board of CCCU in 2017. I did so, in part, due to her desire to better address matters of diversity. During 2019, she and I discussed the four-hundredth anniversary of the Transatlantic

Slave Trade in America and of the need for Christian colleges and universities to engage that reality. This resulted in a panel discussion entitled "American Evolution: Four Hundred Years After the Transatlantic Slave Trade" at the 2020 presidents conference. The panel featured Dr. Bernard Powers Jr., director of the Center for the Study of Slavery at the College of Charleston; Jemar Tisby, executive director of The Witness Foundation; Dr. Michael Battle, former US ambassador to the African Union; and Dr. David Emmanuel Goatley, director of the Office of Black Church Studies at Duke University.

Agency Comes with a Risk that Requires Courage

Initially, Esther refused Mordecai's suggestion, because she felt it would be too risky. Having conducted a personal risk assessment, she concluded there was too much personal risk. Esther's risk was several-fold. The first was that she would have to initiate an audience with the king, she would have to approach King Xerxes when she was not summoned. This is the risk of breaking protocol or disrupting the status quo. She noted that "anyone who appears before the king in his inner court without being invited is doomed to die unless the king holds out his gold scepter. And the king has not called for me to come to him for thirty days" (Esther 4:11, NLT).

Mordecai clued her in to the fact that her being in the position of queen might just be for taking the risk of going to the king. She wouldn't be in the position if the risk were not necessary. It is here that Esther must come to terms with the truth that *exercising agency can include risk of loss, which requires courage.*

The risk of disrupting protocol/status quo is certainly a challenging one. Bubba Wallace of NASCAR fame knows this kind of risk well. While it has gained national prominence, NASCAR is a sport whose roots are in drivers running bootleg whiskey throughout the Appalachians and moonshine in the Southern states.[3] It was and still is one of the conveyors of Southern culture and sensibility. Among its primary symbols has been the Confederate flag. One of the traditions at Darlington (South Carolina) Raceway was a man dressed in Confederate soldier garb carrying the Confederate flag on a pole. The winner would wait for him to get on the hood of his car in victory lane and wave the flag. The tradition was dropped before the 1980s.

Fans waved Confederate flags and wore Confederate flag images on clothing at races. As NASCAR sought to expand beyond the South to the North and West and appeal to more diverse markets, it began to distance itself from Confederate themes, though it did not ban the Confederate flag from being flown in the infield. Not until the death of George Floyd in 2020, did Darrell "Bubba" Wallace, the only African-American driver in NASCAR's top racing series, and supported by Jimmy Johnson and Dale Earnhardt Jr., persuade NASCAR to bar the Confederate flag from its events. They leveraged a combination of personal and positional agency to disrupt and transform NASCAR's status quo.[4]

Another level of risk for Esther was the risk of transparency. Up until now, Esther's racial and cultural identity had been hidden. She was believed to be Persian. Her ascendancy was within the context of a presumed identity. Going to Xerxes on behalf of the Jewish people would not be just an act of solidarity with a marginalized group, it would reveal her true identity. How would King Xerxes respond? She did not know what cost such exposure would bring. At the very least, she could be shunned and dethroned as queen. At the most, she could be executed along with her people.

Hers was the tension between the urgency of the moment and the personal risk tied to exercising her agency for the moment. Resolving the tension would require courage. The exercise of agency includes risk that requires courage. The risk of loss may be personal, reputational, financial, etc. There may be times when it means the risk of losing your job in order to provide an example of integrity and honesty for others. Sometimes, it means risking the prestige to stand up for a principle on behalf of the least and lowly.

Still there are other times when it means losing your very life for the liberty and liberation of others. Moses risked the loss of a peaceful time as a shepherd in Midian to lead Israel out of Egyptian slavery. Harriet Tubman risked the loss of freedom from slavery to lead hundreds of others to escape to freedom. Martin Luther King Jr. risked the loss of a comfortable and prominent ministry in Montgomery to dismantle segregated buses and to captivate the world for the cause of civil rights in America. For Bubba Wallace, it was the risk of death threats and loss of sponsorships. For Jimmy Johnson and Dale Earnhardt Jr., it was the risk of sponsorship, endorsement, and fan-base loss. In each case, they met the risk with courage through the exercise of agency.

Agency Requires Us to See God as the Outcome Securer

Clear of the call to exercise agency, Esther made a request:

> Go, gather together all the Jews who are in Susa, and fast for me. Do not eat or drink for three days, night or day. I and my attendants will fast as you do. When this is done, I will go to the king, even though it is against the law. And if I perish, I perish." (Esther 4:16)

By requesting a fast, Esther demonstrated that she understood the nature of the agency to which she was called. Fasting is a spiritual act, a spiritual discipline. It is bringing cravings of the body under subjection so the spiritual craving for God might be primary and preeminent. In so doing, we demonstrate the sincerity and severity of our quest and hunger for the person, presence, purpose, and plan of God.

By fasting, Esther demonstrated that more than flesh and blood was involved. Her concern was more about needs of the spirit than it was about needs of the body. At stake was not just the survival of some kinsfolk; at stake was the survival of God's people. At stake was the survival of the people out of whom all nations would be blessed. At stake was the survival of the seed of the woman who would bruise the serpent's head. At stake was the plan and program of God. With so much at stake, she could not afford to operate in mere flesh, she needed to operate in spirit. She had to approach the challenge from a spiritual warfare perspective. She called for some people to join her on the level of the spirit.

She fasted because she understood that she needed discernment and courage to do what she needed to do. *In the exercise of agency we must see God as the source of our ability and God as the securer of the outcome.* For the believer, the courage and discernment needed to answer the call to agency comes from God. It was during her three days of fasting that God revealed the strategy and approach she would use with Xerxes and Haman. It was also during that time that God predisposed Xerxes to be open to her approach.

Emboldened and equipped, Esther approached Xerxes and initiated the plan that God had given. She used her personal, practical, and positional agency to protect and deliver her people.

God-directed agency at any level seeks God for what is needed and trusts God to create the conditions of receptivity. Only God can soften hearts. Only God can open and change minds. God secures the outcome when we exercise our agency, because the outcome is tied to a larger work that God has in mind. Esther's exercise of agency was not just to save her people from execution.

It was tied to the furtherance of God's redemptive plan for the world. The ancestral line of Jesus was among those spared.

Likewise God, as the source of our agency and the securer of its outcome, ties our exercise of agency to something far greater than what we see.

Moving Forward with Our Agency

As the clergy met to think through the best way to give voice to what we knew at the time about George Floyd's death, while honoring the initial intention of marking the COVID-19 deaths, White clergy understood the need to be seen and heard acknowledging the pain of the moment as well as the importance of recognizing the continuing problem of that broken racial relationship. They engaged White corporate and community leaders to make a statement, which the *Charlotte Observer* published:

> In the wake of yet one more unjust killing of an unarmed African American, we clergy and community leaders who are white say to our Black neighbors:
>
> We feel outrage, grief, disgust and remorse. We stand with you in the horror, lament and weariness. We're fed up. It's time. We confess our complicity, inertia and timidity. We own our responsibility right now. With God's help, we will change ourselves. With you, we'll change our institutions and our community.[5]

Nearly one hundred names appeared after.

After having made the statement, the question became, How do we give legs and feet to it? Many have given themselves to an ongoing process of awareness, ownership, and agency individually and collectively. This is what God calls us to.

Chapter 11

CREATING OPPORTUNITY: KHARY BRIDGEWATER'S MISSION TO INSPIRE EQUITY

Mac

Living in impoverished communities is difficult enough, but add in a global crisis, and difficult becomes nearly impossible. Such was the case during the COVID-19 pandemic. And some of the hardest hit places in those communities were some of the most essential to the health of them. According to *Bloomberg News:*

> The Covid-19 economic shutdown has hurt African-American businesses the most among racial and ethnic groups in the US, with a 41% decline of black owners from February to April, a new study from the National Bureau of Economic Research shows. While the pandemic hit entrepreneurs across the board, closing some 3.3 million small businesses at least temporarily, the sidelining of 440,000 African Americans was especially severe. Black owners may have fared worse because fewer

of them operated in industries deemed "essential" during the pandemic.[1]

Add to that George Floyd's murder, where police officer Derek Chauvin knelt on his neck and back for nine minutes and twenty-nine seconds during an arrest. The summer of 2020 was a sea of social response in dozens of cities across the United States from diverse racial communities.

As Khary Bridgewater, senior program officer for the DeVos Family Foundations in Grand Rapids, Michigan, assisting churches, watched, he felt the pain the people in those communities were experiencing. Not only had he grown up in a similar African-American community, he had been studying the challenges of African-American communities since his university days.

Khary grew up in Saginaw, Michigan, which had the country's highest homicide rate in communities of more than forty thousand. Getting into trouble in Saginaw would have been easy. But amid that environment, he was shaped by his parents' faith. At the age of five, he walked down the aisle at his Missionary Baptist church to go to the altar and accept Jesus into his life. As he was walking, he felt a hand on his shoulder. "I thought it was my mother's hand, but when I looked, nobody was there," he says. "I later realized it was the Holy Spirit's presence on my life. I have always had this sense of the Lord sheltering me and pulling me back from dangerous places."

Khary always had a sense of living in two worlds—the world of his Black suburb and the world where White culture was dominant. Because of living in these two worlds, he felt compelled to become a bridge-builder. First between the Black and White communities and later between the church and the broader society. In particular, he knew that bridge-building work included creating a connection between diverse racial groups. God gave Khary the burden and understanding to be effective in interpreting each racial community to the other.

Alongside the influence of his parents, Khary attributes his development as a bridge-builder in part to the contribution of White influences. He felt grateful for people like Sister Beata Bugala, his kindergarten teacher, and Daniel Sealey, one of his science teachers who nurtured his research in science fairs and stimulated his love for science, which eventually led him to attend the Massachusetts Institute of Technology (MIT) to study mechanical and ocean engineering. "When people love you, that creates an imprint on your life," he says. "I realized that I could never walk away from White people because I experienced people who loved me."

Filled with big hopes and dreams, after he graduated high school, he excitedly left the violence of his hometown and headed to college in the Boston area. But the violence and struggle followed him, as he learned that thirteen family members died about the same time, including two who were murdered. Khary's world began to crumble. "I had escaped the violence of Saginaw and was at college in MIT, but I was drowning in depression because of all the death in my family," he admits. "I was disoriented and lost while trying to navigate a new and challenging environment."

During these difficult times, he sought solace from God and became involved with the Black church and InterVarsity on campus. But vulnerable communities kept coming to his mind, and he knew that something had to change—he had to take ownership and allow that to move him into action.

While attending MIT and eventually transferring to Boston University, Khary was shaped by the teaching and scholarship of professors Peter Senge, who authored *The Fifth Discipline,* and Michael Porter, a professor from Harvard. Their research helped

Khary began to think critically about how to solve complex problems in social systems.

One of the complex problems facing Boston was gang violence. Having come from a violent city, Khary was eager to apply his understanding-of-systems thinking to solve social problems in the city of Boston. His opportunity came when a friend asked him to take over the consulting arm of the Emmanuel Gospel Center (EGC), a faith-based nonprofit organization with a robust church network working together to impact the city.

One of the Emmanuel Gospel Center's partnerships was with the Ten Point Coalition, founded by Eugene Rivers, Bruce Wall, and Ray Hammond. The coalition was built through an alliance of pastors, researchers, police officers, and the courts to address the problems of violence and disenfranchisement of young Black men. The work of this coalition was so effective that it brought gang violence to a standstill with no teen murders for twenty-nine months ending in 1998. The "Boston Miracle," as it was referred to, also saw the overall Boston homicide rate decline by 63 percent.[2] It made such an impact that even *Newsweek* and the *Guardian* covered the story that June.

In his research, Khary worked with the Ten Point Coalition, Black Ministerial Alliance, and Harvard University's Youth Violence Prevention Center to create predictive models of gang violence. He discovered that traumatic stress is one of the clearest predictors of community violence because these factors subconsciously predispose those who suffer from these conditions to aggressively startle responses, which can trigger violent interactions. Khary also learned that economic disparity between groups of people who live in close proximity is one of the highest predictors of community violence. Therefore young people who live in areas that have high violence or where income disparity exists are likely to be victims and perpetrators of violence.[3]

Khary realized that an important antidote to gang violence was to provide employment to African-American young people. Jobs provided income as well as space for young people to cool off amid retaliatory cycles. Young people who had less unstructured time, due to employment obligations, became less violent.

He felt empowered by the knowledge he gained and was ready to return to his home state to apply it there.

Back to Michigan

Khary returned to Michigan in 2010 and went to work for the DeVos Family Foundations, helping urban churches build congregational programs to serve families and children in Michigan. Over the next eleven years, he built a network of churches and institutions to address the needs of their community. In addition, he worked as an adjunct professor at Cornerstone University's Grand Rapids Theological Seminary.

When COVID-19 hit in full force in early 2020, the alliance that Khary had been building addressed the needs of the minority community. The church network was able to interface with the medical community in Kent County, Michigan. They implemented strategies regarding in-person church closings, masking, and social distancing, and they have now met weekly for more than eighteen months. For a season, their work lowered the incidences of COVID among Blacks and Hispanics, seeing the elimination of racial disparities in COVID infection rates for all of Kent County. In contrast, across the rest of Michigan, African Americans were experiencing three to six times the mortality rates of Whites, due to COVID-19.[4]

As the work continued, heightened in urgency by the social unrest and devastation, Khary began to cast a vision for the future. He called it a Marshall Plan for the African-American community.

Inspire Equity

In 1948 Secretary of State George Marshall introduced the European Recovery Program to assist Western Europe after the devastation of World War II. The plan raised $15 billion to help finance rebuilding efforts on the European continent. Thanks to the plan's efforts, from 1948–1953 Europe achieved the greatest period of economic activity in its history as European economies exceeded pre-war levels. Pragmatically the Marshal Plan helped prevent starvation and the expansion of communism in Western Europe. The plan represented 2.5 percent of United States GDP invested in that region.

Khary cast a similar vision to impact African-American communities over the next decade, fueled not by politics, but by a biblical vision for human life and its flourishing. To that end, Khary formed Norstell Capital, with his colleague Andrew Sims, a private investment and management firm seeking to stimulate minority-owned businesses. Norstell is positioning itself to address needs that he has been studying for thirty years.

The ten-year goal is to move $500 billion in capital into African-American communities through private equity and private debt. This is a private-sector solution to create an inclusive economy. After ten years, Khary hopes to see parity where Blacks own businesses at the same rate as Whites own businesses.

Movement.org and the Conference of National Black Churches (CNBC) quickly came on board as national allies, offering help, support, and visibility. CNBC represents the largest seven African-American denominations and 47 percent of the African-American community. Both partners created multiple conversations and worked with him to cultivate a long-term vision for justice. They also connected Khary with invaluable introductions to leaders and other partners with expertise. For instance, they are working (as of the time of this writing) to finalize arrangements with the National Association of Black Accountants. And several prominent business and financial leaders have stepped in to serve on Norstell's advisory board, including Bob Doll (board chair of Movement.org, chief investment officer of Crossmark, and formerly chief equity strategist with BlackRock), Mark Linsz (former treasurer at Bank of America), and Dr. Barron Harvey (dean emeritus of Howard University).

When Khary first approached Movement.org and me about this idea, I eagerly made introductions to city leaders across the United States. One of the first introductions was to Claude for the city of Charlotte. Charlotte is home to Bank of America, which has set aside $2 billion to invest in minority businesses. Through a series of conversations, Khary engaged the mayor of Charlotte and several leaders in the financial industry. He also brought Claude on board to chair a local advisory team to architect the strategy for Charlotte. Because of Charlotte's strategic financial center and Claude's three decades of leadership, this synergistic relationship has created momentum for the city.

I also introduced him to Eric Thompson (Eric's leadership role in Norfolk is described in chapter 7). Through Eric's firm at UBS, Eric in turn made introductions to a former professional athlete. Khary developed a strategy to have professional athletes become ambassadors for minority business ownership (see chapter 7).

Other city conversations are happening in Grand Rapids, Indianapolis, and Dallas. In addition to Bank of America and UBS, other institutions who have joined in the conversation have been Wells Fargo and Morgan Stanley.

Khary clarifies that the monies they are raising and giving to the communities are being done in two ways. The majority of the money is being invested in Black businesses and a complimentary set of resources are being donated to Black churches and nonprofits. "This is a practical set of concentrated investments in fifty cities over the next five years," he says. "We want to be in five cities in 2021 and prepping for the next five cities."

His vision's methodology is to build multiracial advisory groups in each city that will identify and recommend for investment businesses that will increase employment opportunities in minority communities. Norstell Capital will identify sources of capital (investment banks, local investors, governmental) that can be bundled to provide the working capital needed to accelerate the work of a qualified business.

By 2022 the plan is to solidify the advisory councils in the first ten cities, to connect two hundred businesses to the strategy, and then to execute on purchases. The conviction, Khary believes, is that investors will want to invest in their own backyards.

The Church's Role

Khary sees an important role for the church to play—especially churches that worship outside of these disenfranchised communities. He saw the US church show up in great action during the height of the COVID shutdowns, as he, in his work with the DeVos Family Foundation, partnered with Churches Helping Churches and Justin Giboney of the AND Campaign. Giboney had a vision of more affluent churches providing $3,000 to $5,000 grants to smaller, inner-city churches who would be helped by microgrants to sustain operations for a month or two. The campaign successfully assisted hundreds of churches with $1.2 million in raised funds. Of that total, Khary led the Michigan churches into raising $500,000.

"The role of the White church is to be an ally, to make the case that justice is biblical and practical," Khary says. "An important part of justice is restitution so doing justice involves writing checks and investing. Justice takes shackles off economically.

This creates a spiritual framework and is ministry driven, coming out of Christian witness. God has asked us to do this, to lead people to Christ."

The Black church is the heartbeat of the strategy and its core communicator. It provides haven for those families who have suffered. "The civil rights movement was about legislation," he says. "This is an economic movement and a church movement."

As Khary considers the relationship between his work and the Micah 6:8 imperative, he says, "We often think about race and justice as optional parts of our faith. We view our primary dimension of faith as our personal relationship with God, which is absolutely true. We enter three realities simultaneously: we are children of God, members of the body of Christ, and members of God's kingdom. God has set up an intentional government where He intends us to interact with other believers across racial lines. Being part of a spiritual family comes with responsibilities toward the rest of the family.

"God requires justice from us. There is not an option. Humility is setting aside the trappings of privilege. We are called to serve with our privilege and to show mercy. Justice is important as millions of lives have been destroyed by racial injustice."

Khary is modeling for us what it means to show civility, empathy, and pragmatism in demonstrating our faith. God's invitation is to look at each member in the body of Christ across racial lines through the lens of family. We are one blood. We are God's new society together.

Chapter 12

ELEPHANTS AND
THE UNFINISHED TASK

The integrity and strength of any relationship is determined by the ability to address the elephants in the room. As that is the case with relationships, so is it the case with this book that comes out of the relationship between the two of us. The course of the past five years has been one of discussion and discovery. It is no accident that the past five years have been the context for our increased discussions, because during those five years we have seen violence and hatred become more pronounced.

Below we share one of the many ongoing discussions we have. This one, in particular, is about defending each other as one community of faith.

Our prayer is that it will ignite within you a desire to pursue your own discussions to lead to awareness, to ownership, and ultimately to using your agency to make a lasting change.

The Unfinished Task of Place

CLAUDE: Throughout our history, there have been White Christians of extreme courage—especially from the period of abolition to the Civil Rights Movement. In fact, during the Freedom Rides, there were White Christians who put their lives on the line to defend Blacks and to spark real change.

Having said that, what many White Christians do not often understand is that many Southern White Christians—as well as some Northerners—used the Bible and a version of Christianity to justify enslaving people. In fact, a lot of people don't realize how deeply ingrained the issue of slavery is within our denominations. Wherever we see the word *Southern* attached to a denomination, that comes out of that discussion of slavery. So, for instance, we can look at the history of the Baptist church. A split took place within the denomination. Those who were anti-slavery became the American Baptists. Those who were pro-slavery formed their own denomination, which was the birth of the Southern Baptist Convention.

Blacks who adopted Christianity were able to interpret Scripture for themselves, and having done so, across the years, then had to defend Christianity against the enslavement and racism of White Christians. And in having to defend Christianity itself, they often found themselves defending White Christians, regardless of whether or not those White Christians protected or defended them. So to Black Christians, that sense of unity as one community of faith has not been their experience on the whole.

MAC: Can you give an example scripturally?

CLAUDE: From Genesis 1, we see a pattern in the creation in which we see the phrase repeated, "according to their various kinds." But when it comes to the creation of humanity, that phrase isn't there. Instead we see "in the image and likeness of God." There is no "according to their various kinds" difference; it is just the one "in the image and likeness of God," the *imago Dei*.

From the very beginning, we realize that our equality, our equal status, is found in us being created in God's image and likeness. We are all image bearers.

Then in Genesis 2, what does God do? God places Adam in a garden. So part of this image bearing is having place. Right? Both Adam and Eve had *place*, they had community. They had relationship with each other. So God's created intention is to have place and to be in community. Anything that denies that goes against the intention of God and, therefore, must be called sin.

But then, the Africans and their descendants carefully identified with the exodus: "Let my people go." And they identified with the prophets and their calls for justice, whether it was Amos or Isaiah or Micah. And then they looked at the Gospels and at Jesus, who said, "The Spirit of the Lord is on me, because he has anointed me to proclaim good news to the poor. He has sent me to proclaim freedom for the prisoners and recovery of sight for the blind, to set the oppressed free." And so there is this thread throughout Scripture that the African and his and her descendants latched onto.

What we know as the Black church arose out of a protest against the denial of place and personhood within the White church.

MAC: The truth is we all need to realize that from a biblical perspective, people who claim their identity in the Person of Jesus are now part of one family, and therefore we need to look at these challenges through the lens of family. The unity of the church must come by embracing it in all its racial expression. It is what gives the gospel credibility and believability in the world. Historically we have not done this very well. Especially when we look at the birth of the AME [African Methodist Episcopal] church and other expressions of the African-American community who felt there was no place for them inside the way the White church was expressing itself.

I think we must wrestle with that. We must own that. We have to take necessary steps to address it, if we're going to live up to the standard that God has for us and look at it through that lens of family. In a sense we have two very real conversions: a conversion to the Person of Jesus and a conversion to the people of Jesus. It is that second conversion that is missing in far too many places. The absence of that second conversion has produced a blind spot within the church.

CLAUDE: Elena Aronson, the director of training for Arrabon seconds your sentiment. In an April 27, 2021, Barna report, "Discipling toward Racial Justice: A Q&A with Elena Aronson," she says, "I think this will require a new type of conversion: a movement from caring about personal moral responsibility to responsibility for those outside your direct social circle and the social, economic and political implications that come as a result. Leaders can spark theses conversions through the messages they preach, the songs they use in worship, the art they create and the way they engage in outreach and missions."[1]

Paul seeks to prompt that second conversion in Philemon. Paul addresses this letter not just to Philemon, but also to those who gather in his house for worship. Hence, this is a corrective letter to a body of believers who worship in a place where slaves are owned. From it, Paul addresses several blind spots. The first is the blind spot of recognizing the essential personhood of all people. Paul employs personal language about Onesimus that affirms his humanity. By doing so, he inherently challenges the treatment of him that denies his personhood.

The second is the blind spot of recognizing all believers in Christ as brothers and sisters. Paul calls Onesimus *brother*. As a member in the new family of Jesus, Onesimus has equal status before them as one of the redeemed.

The standards of the family of Jesus critique the standards of the world. It reshapes the lines of relating to those with whom we come in contact in the neighborhood, how we judge those we see on the elevator, the compassion and empathy we might possess for the person we see on the street. The recognition of someone as our brother or sister in the Lord should reconfigure the second thought, the benefit of the doubt, or even the grace we extend to one who is in the family of Jesus.

The third blind spot is the calculus of human value. By calling Onesimus a beloved brother and assistant, Paul challenges their sense of valuation. Onesimus' value as a person, as a beloved brother, as a carrier of the gospel, as a fellow worker in the Lord's church is far greater than the profit gathered and the expenses reduced from his free labor among them. The worth of the human person, the value of membership in the family of God, and the usefulness in the kingdom of God far outweigh any consideration that one gives to maximized profits through economic exploitation and manipulation. The calculus of human value is at the very core of our faith. It is found in the love of God for us all. That's why it's so important for us to defend each other, to collaborate, to give honor and recognize that we all have that place in the family.

So let's look at what happened in Charleston, South Carolina, in 2015 in which a White man entered a historic Black church and shot and killed Christians. People came together and intentionally pursued cross-cultural relationships. By the following year, by the intense atmosphere of the political landscape and the presidential election, many White Christians failed to show up and respond to what was taking place.

Black Christians were saying, "Hey, this is a problem. This

needs to be spoken to." But when White Christians were not defending and protecting their brothers and sisters, the silence caused Blacks to get the message, *You are on your own.*

It intensified the feeling of isolation, of abandonment, of betrayal. And it caused many Black Christians to question how true or how genuine the response to Charleston was in the first place.

In 2016, during a period of unrest, a prominent White pastor told me, "I'd like to say something about it but I can't." And I said, "Why not?" He said, "My top givers will not get with this." This pastor has Black people in his church. But he was not willing to make them feel safe, because he does not want to make this other group feel uncomfortable. He is an example of how too often we make Whites comfortable at the expense of Blacks' discomfort.

The Unfinished Task of Privilege

MAC: Historically, I think one of the root issues for White Christians is that we have a tendency to compartmentalize. We compartmentalize faith as a part of life, and then to a whole different compartment we place how we view issues of race and economics.

CLAUDE: You know, people call this word a grenade, but really, the ability to "compartmentalize" is a privilege. When we think about voting, healthcare, law enforcement, in many respects, it is a privilege to be able to think of those as simple political issues. Right? Because from the place where one sits as a majority, you have always had the right to vote. You have always had access to healthcare. The police have always treated you well, because their official role was never to keep you in place but to protect your place. But for people of color, it has not been an idea to be debated. It's life itself. So compartmentalizing just isn't an option.

It was looking at these things, which are matters of life and death, from the claims of the gospel, and being infused by the power of the Spirit and the courage that prayer brings to be able to engage and to stay engaged against what had been generational odds against them.

And therefore, it's not just, *This is a matter of life and death,* as opposed to compartmentalized object for debate; it is the approach to it and the engagement of it through the claims of Scripture.

MAC: Life or death? In what ways?

CLAUDE: In the course of addressing the issues surrounding race, some are prone to say that it is political and use that as a reason not to engage. The ability to view these issues as simply political is from the position of not being threatened by them, and/or protected by them. White supremacy and white supremacists can be a topic of debate and political manipulation for some, but they are an existential threat for people of color and Jews. White supremacy, "the belief that the white race is inherently superior to other races and that white people should have control over people of other races," was the animating principle behind Dylan Roof's shooting spree, which killed the pastor and eight congregants in Mother Emanuel AME Church in Charleston, South Carolina, in 2015, and Robert Bowers' mass shooting at the Tree of Life Synagogue in Squirrel Hill, Pennsylvania, killing eleven people and wounding six in 2018. It is a matter of life and death.

The extension of the Voting Rights Act can be a topic of debate by people who have always had access to voting and never needed the protection of the Act's enforcement in order to be counted. But for those who were denied it for 189 years and continue to face challenges in the exercising of it, it is not political.

It is life and death. People gave their lives in order for it to be attained. Because so much of what affects the lives of people is tied to voting, it is a matter of life and death.

MAC: The sad reality is that many White Christians simply are not aware. We don't defend because we don't necessarily see the need to or that it's important even in today's world to stand united and defend our Black brothers and sisters in Christ.

White privilege is often a misunderstood phrase. What White Christians need to understand is that we are not on a level playing field with many communities of color. There are consequences to historic disadvantages. I have often been struck by the sheer historic weight of 345 years passing between the arrival of the first slaves in 1619 to the passage of Civil Rights legislation in 1964. That represents *seventeen* generations of disadvantage. As a White Christian I need to look at current circumstances through this historical lens.

What Paul appeals to in 2 Corinthian 8:13 is "equality" or "fairness." We are generous toward one another out of an ethic of love for fellow family members. God's primary desire is not for us to feel guilt over our current circumstance but to assume our agency for the benefit of others who have less opportunity. Jesus becomes our model—that through His poverty we might become rich. We have such an extraordinary opportunity to "make others rich" and to manifest the fruit of being converted to the primacy of unity in pragmatic, life-giving ways. Jesus is inviting us into greater Christlikeness to enter the suffering of others. That is why the story of the Good Samaritan is so powerful and so important. What makes Christianity Christianity is the Incarnation. Jesus among us. He is inviting us into the world and to enter His suffering for the world. One application of that suffering is to alleviate the pain of others in the spirit of equality.

Claude: The day after the 2016 election, my middle-school daughter, Carsyn, came home from school in tears. My wife and I asked her, "What's wrong?" And she told us about what some White kids began to say to her Hispanic friends. "You're about to be sent back." These were middle-school kids, who days prior had not said these things to Hispanic kids, but the day *after* felt both the liberty and the necessity to say it.

Hearing my daughter tell us that, took me right back to my own childhood when a kid called me the "N" word.

How do middle-school kids get that? They get what they hear from their parents. And so, in this environment, people of color felt threatened. And imagine being that Hispanic child's mother or father and asking how your child's day went and that being what that parent heard.

Mac: I think that the ethos of White evangelicalism is that faith is very private. If we have a friend who is minority, we feel empathy and concern for that friend because we understand this environment is difficult. At the same time, we do not necessarily have the perceived ability that we can make a change regarding this larger national conversation. I think that is where a lot of thoughtful White Christians struggle, because we are not quite sure what to do. We are concerned about the issue. But we also feel a sense of helplessness in knowing what to do and how to influence opinion.

Claude: One of the points of clarification or distinction is that faith is personal but not private. Biblical faith has a very public dimension. We are called to be light and salt, which is quite public. And for those you've described, I think that unless there is necessity that creates urgency, there is not the move to exercise agency. Right? Hence why that nine-minute video of George Floyd's killing was so crucial. Because at that moment in seeing it, you had an experience. That George Floyd video took everybody immediately to the urgency. We all had the experience and were saying, "No, no, no. This is wrong, and something must be done. Something has to be said."

MAC: As we are talking, it feels like to defend each other, we're really talking about three themes. One is the historic denial of personhood and how we need to understand that historically. Two is the reality of disparity that communities of color are experiencing. And three is the theological value of this unity of the church.

CLAUDE: You're exactly right. When thinking about the ways we use the term *evangelical*, we must recognize the shift from evangelical as an adjective to evangelical as a noun. As an adjective, the stress was on Christian/Christianity. As a noun, the focus became a group, a power bloc. As a bloc, it is easy for it to become an idol that is open to manipulation and absent of critique. As an adjective, it is checked and critiqued by the noun, *Christianity*. As it is possible to be more Baptist than Christian, it is also possible to be more evangelical than Christian.

One of the forces with which we must come to terms is the southernization of the church. By southernization, I mean the process whereby distinctive cultural forms associated with the American South spread to other regions of the United States. John Egerton wrote of this in his book *The Americanization of Dixie*. He notes that religion was one of the elements of Southern culture that had a discernible impact on the wider society. As much as that is true, it is also true that Southern culture had a profound impact upon religion, particularly evangelical religion.

MAC: In what ways?

CLAUDE: Southernized Christianity demands obedience, conformity, intolerance, the subjugation of women, and a White purity culture. They may not come right out and say these things, but the actions are there.

This southernization began as southerners moved west. They took their "peculiar institution" of slavery with them or tried to. Oklahoma and Arizona are perfect examples. Blacks were freer when Oklahoma was a territory than when it became a state. With statehood came southernization. Once they were granted statehood, the first legislature wrote segregation into law. What is now Arizona was originally part of the territory of New Mexico, until the southern part seceded from the Union to form the Territory of Arizona and was organized by the Confederate States of America. Oregon was the only state to enter the Union as a free state but with a Black exclusion law—which meant that Whites couldn't have slaves there, but Blacks couldn't live there.

The role of southernized Christianity in the immediate aftermath of the Civil War was about restoring Southern pride and dignity by creating a false narrative that the war had been part of God's grand design. They did not see slavery as sinful and made no apology for it. The churches were bastions of regional identity. They were less about what it means to be a citizen of the kingdom and more about what it meant to be a White southerner. We see that continuing today.

The Unfinished Task of Price

MAC: So what's the answer to Black Christians' and White Christians' desire to collaborate and better reflect unity?

CLAUDE: As it relates to Black Christians being collaborative, for some it's having the courage to risk being disappointed. And then to engage. That is the fundamental thing, because for some, the disappointment causes them to think, *I can do this on my own*. For example, Black Christians may say, "You want us to come to a prayer rally? You've so disappointed us, there's no need for us to join you. We can pray on our own."

MAC: It's an interesting dynamic I've noticed down through the years that one of the challenges for White leaders is that oftentimes we invite leaders of color to meetings who wouldn't come and then we aren't invited to their meetings. That is a bit of a generalization, but I think for White leaders, we really have to be intentional about building the relationship one leader at a time and to commit to whatever length of time it will take to build a reservoir of trust to move beyond the relationship into whatever other involvement or activity is going to look like.

It is difficult to overcome, in some cases, decades of mistrust. And it requires a lot of intention around that. There is no substitute for just showing up.

CLAUDE: What you just said is so very important. For Black Christians, in general, we have a form of PTSD. The personal and the collective experience of racism presents a level of wounding. And that necessitates a guardedness and a hermeneutic of suspicion. *Can I really trust you? Are you really real? Is this genuine? How long will it last?* All of the questions come out of a wounding experience relationally. All of these are things to which Blacks are prone in dealing with Whites, Christian or not. And so, yes, it's really about showing up with consistency.

And yet it is our calling, our necessity, for both of us to persist to build bridges despite the extraordinarily challenging environment in which we find ourselves. I do it out of a sense of call, a response to the claim that Christ has placed on me. I also do it out of an experience of authentic and genuine friendship, which I have had. And so where and when I may experience a slight or disappointment, I'm able to pull from these other relationships, and say, but Mac. But Doug. But Leighton. But Bob.

Another thing I've learned is what I'd call *understanding different equalizations*. This is a term used in sound editing and mixing. There are a variety of sets you can adjust by raising or lowering to get the sound that is particular to you. One's individual/social context influences what the presets are in terms of the volume of certain tones. No one's equalization is exactly the same. If we don't realize that, when we encounter someone whose equalization is different from ours, we make certain assumptions about them, such as what is particularly loud in our equalization is not even in their set, when it may be in their set but just at a lower frequency.

MAC: There is also a sense of entering into God's concern for disadvantaged communities, for just the sheer level of brokenness in the world, and really, in a sense, part of my own spiritual development is entering into God's concern and using whatever abilities and agency I have to make a difference.

CLAUDE: It helps explain the response of those families whose loved ones were killed in Charleston. When they stood in that courtroom, not expecting to say anything, and the judge said, "Do you have something to say?" and they said, "I forgive you." Where did that come from? Part of it was aspiration—what the Bible calls *hope*. Even though they weren't feeling it, they spoke as what was true for them in that moment, that desire. Because for them and for many, there are only two options—aspiration or despair. Aspiration promotes engagement. Despair promotes resignation, disengagement, and a consumption of anger and bitterness. And so they could not—and I cannot—give in to despair. That's not an option.

We still have an unfinished task. We have come so far, yet still we have more to do.

Chapter 13

WHAT'S NEXT?

Every person has a racial story. Every solution begins with a conversation. This book is about marrying those two truths, through the lens of Micah 6:8—to do justly, to love mercy, and to walk humbly with God.

Our hope is that as we have discussed what this entails, you have found yourself convicted. But more than that, encouraged and motivated—for the gospel is Good News! And that Good News brings real hope and reality for change.

Now the question becomes: What are we going to do about it?

We have highlighted the issues, and we dare not leave you without some practical ways to get started.

Awareness

My (Mac's) journey into awareness took place primarily through encountering African Americans in the New York City context. God was gracious to my wife, Marya, and me, as I described in chapter 2, through the hospitality of the Caesar family. Relationships are always birthed primarily by showing up. That may seem obvious, but we cannot overstate the importance of initiative and intention. Because we showed up in New York City, God used that initiative to introduce us to the Caesars who would forever change us through their generosity.

For our first six years in New York City, showing up at African-American churches and connecting with African-American leaders on their turf was incredibly meaningful and important. This was equally true as I met and connected with Latin leaders, Asian leaders, and other White leaders.

Awareness must begin with a strategy of showing up. A person can identify a church or organization that invites assistance in some form (volunteerism, donations) and then participate. Many cities host MLK observances or Juneteenth observances where a person can attend and meet people. God has already prepared someone you can befriend and learn from. The learning will be mutual.

An equally important part of awareness is having a strategy to learn about the other. I (Mac) shared in chapter 2 how formational the book *Roots* was in my own journey. Wherever you find the opportunity to learn through reading and museum experiences, you will find them critically important. On my trips to Rwanda, I have taken hundreds of leaders to visit genocide memorials there. In Kigali, the National Genocide Memorial has 250,000 persons buried on the premises. It is through studying that we become fluent with the historical and contemporary context of diverse communities. Those annual visits to East Africa and learning about the Rwandan genocide helped motivate our travel colleagues to sponsor eleven thousand children. My wife and I have sponsored twenty children in Rwanda today.

As much as possible, it is good to become a student of other cultures and their experiences.

We learn through stories. One African-American pastoral colleague, Gary Frost, had a congregation in Youngstown, Ohio, and he described the wailing of mothers who attended the funerals of their sons killed violently in their city in the late 1980s and early 1990s. Gary described the experience of walking through the Youngstown cemetery with his twenty-three-year-old son, Timothy, who counted off the tombstones of forty young friends. Gary said his son told him that he just had to stop counting, since it was too depressing. This is the experience of many ravaged communities in urban America and parts of the globe.

Having these kinds of conversations with others of a different race will grow our empathy and open your eyes to a sobering and yet powerful awareness.

What Do We Need to Be More Aware Of?

We can only love that which we know. As you start your journey, ask God to give you an unyielding awareness of where His heart lies for the most vulnerable. Then ask yourself these questions:

- What do I see when I look inwardly?
- Where and when has it been difficult for me to show humility?
- In what ways can I better walk humbly before God?
- What level of historical, contemporary, and spiritual awareness do I have of the racial matters that plague my city/community?
- In what ways might God be calling me to confess and repent?

As you ponder the answers, consider opening your eyes and minds to the following:

- The demographics of your city along population, racial, and socioeconomic lines

- The great "stubborn facts" of your city—single-parent homes, incarceration rates, graduation rates, income disparity
- Where God is stirring to foster unity and hope from the church across racial lines
- The local heroes in your city

But don't stop there. Read. Here is a brief list to get you started:

American Original Sin: Racism, White Privilege, and the Bridge to a New America by Jim Wallis

At Canaan's Edge: America in the King Years, 1965–1968 by Taylor Branch

Beyond Liberation: The Gospel in the Black American Experience by Carl Ellis

Caste: The Origins of Our Discontents by Isabel Wilkerson

The Color of Law: A Forgotten History of How Our Government Segregated America by Richard Rothstein

Faithful Antiracism by Chad Brennan and Dr. Christina Edmondson

Giants: The Parallel Lives of Fredrick Douglass and Abraham Lincoln by John Stauffer

Ghosts in the Room by Dr. Glenn Bracey

The Grand Betrayal by Dr. Michael O. Emerson and Dr. Glenn Bracey

How the Word Is Passed: A Reckoning with the History of Slavery Across America by Clint Smith

The Immortal Life of Henrietta Lacks by Rebeca Skloot

Just Mercy: A Story of Justice and Redemption by Bryan Stephenson

Letters to a Birmingham Jail: A Response to the Words and

Dreams of Dr. Martin Luther King Jr. by Bryan Lorrits, editor

The Presumption of Guilt: The Arrest of Henry Louis Gates Jr. and Race, Class, and Crime in America by Charles Ogletree

The Roadmap to Reconciliation 2.0: Moving Communities into Unity, Wholeness, and Justice by Brenda Salter McNeil

Roots: The Saga of an American Family by Alex Haley

Also, watch movies and have discussions with a biracial group. Let these start you off:

Belle
The Best of Enemies
The Birth of a Nation
Blood Done Sign My Name
Emanuel
The Green Book
The Hate U Give
The Help
Just Mercy
Son of the South

Awareness always comes with education. So commit to educating yourself—and then others. Too many of us are woefully ignorant of history in terms of the depth and extent of domestic terror, neglect, etc., that has occurred within our country. Many of our contemporary issues are outgrowths of the unreconciled past. The current concern about the various voting laws being passed by state legislatures comes from the remembrance of laws that restricted and denied Black voting as a backlash to Reconstruction. Another example is the tension between law enforcement and communities of color. Many of my (Claude's) White colleagues and friends do not understand the depth of pain and distrust African Americans have toward law enforcement.

But when they begin to study history, awareness dawns to a new understanding. They learn that from the time African slaves were first sold to hundreds of years later when the Civil Rights Act became law, the role of law enforcement, especially Southern law enforcement, was geared toward reinforcing the status of Africans and later African Americans as property, and later as a deprived, denigrated, and subjugated class of people. It was law enforcement's role to keep the Negro in his or her place. Some White law enforcement officers were also either active members or silent supporters of such groups as the Red Shirts, the White League, state Democratic Rifle Clubs, and the Ku Klux Klan.

The images of Sheriffs Bull Connor and Jim Clark in Birmingham and Selma actively leading law enforcement officers in beating and fire hosing unarmed Blacks and Whites whose only crime was the peaceful pursuit of justice are seared into African-American communities' collective memory.

One must not forget that federal troops had to be brought in to protect Black children who were involved in school desegregation. The local police could not be trusted with the task. In most communities, Black police officers only policed Black neighborhoods. That was believed to be their place. With the Equal Opportunity Employment Act of 1972, while the overall face of policing began to change as people of color mainstreamed into citywide policing, the underlying attitudes, assumptions, and orientation had not changed. It would take a much longer time for that to happen. Furthermore, while persons of color and women gained admission into the wider force, a glass ceiling kept them from the levels of leadership where substantive cultural change could take place.

So when African Americans express concern over the trustworthiness of law enforcement, correctly or incorrectly, education of that piece of history can help us understand why they would feel that way.

Spiritual awareness can come by encouraging vision and values formation with cross-congregational work, such as pulpit exchanges; shared service projects and worship experiences; and using arts, movies, and literature to foster increased dialogue and understanding. As awareness grows, the church becomes more unabashed in its proclamation of the kingdom of God and the shalom of God. Just as we create safe spaces for people investigating God and faith, so we can create safe spaces for people to wrestle with the difficulty of owning communal sin, repentance, and responsibility.

Ownership

We move from theory toward action when we own what needs to be done. Gary Frost and his wife, Lynette, are two of my (Mac's) great heroes. Not only did Gary pastor in Youngstown, Ohio, he was also the highest-ranking minority in the Southern Baptist Convention in 2001 when named as a vice president. He was on the front page of *USA Today* in 1995 when he accepted an apology on behalf of the denomination for its racist roots. Gary walks the talk.

He has been an extraordinary bridge-builder for the past four decades between communities of color and White communities. And he and Lynette have "owned" the plight of fatherlessness, having fostered forty-six children over the course of their marriage. Gary and Lynette's hearts have been moved with a profound sense of mercy toward the fatherless. Their sense of ownership was rooted in God's mercy toward orphans.

I became familiar with the Frosts when they moved to New York City after Gary assumed the position as director of the Metro New York Baptist Association. He and Lynette were involved in many of Movement.org's initiatives, including our work in Africa.

I remember one trip when Lynette traveled with me to East Africa on a World Vision trip. She told me the story of their last adopted child, Ben. Even though the Frosts had been fostering for many years, and were getting older, Gary felt like God wanted them to take one more child. So when Lynette got a call from the hospital that a baby boy had been born and did not have a family to go home to, she asked Gary what he thought they could do. Gary said, "Bring him home. His name is Ben."

The Frosts have been such a remarkable couple and friends that I have asked Gary to speak at my funeral if he outlives me. Gary has embodied Jesus as well as anyone I have met on the planet.

Ownership creates within us a deep longing for those needing mercy to experience God's mercy.

Becoming Merciful

Mercy begins with a reflection on God's mercy toward us. Consider the truth of Romans 5:8: "God demonstrates his own love for us in this: While we were still sinners, Christ died for us." Even when we were ignorant and indifferent, God took the initiative to meet our needs in His mercy. The more we apprehend this mercy, the more we will be moved to be merciful.

Ask yourself, "Where and when has it been difficult for me to show mercy? Why? How does that reflect the ways God has shown me mercy?"

In addition to reflecting on God's mercy, pray for the great needs of individuals and communities. While in North India in 1983, the team and I (Mac) prayed for three to nine hours every Friday for the vast communities of the spiritually and physically poor. Investing that kind of time can only increase our hearts. It increased mine with a great burden for that region to this day.

Mercy also arises when we make the effort to become proximate to the need, as I (Claude) discussed in chapter 8 about the Good Samaritan. If you aren't close to the needs, it becomes more difficult to experience mercy and ownership. That is one of the reasons I got involved in the Community Building Initiative and it's one of the reasons Mac found it important to immerse himself in communities across New York City and increasingly around the globe. Once we see and feel the needs of others, we cannot but be moved to do something about that need.

- Where might you be challenged to reach beyond the limits of comfort?
- With whom or in what area might you need to achieve greater proximity or get a close-up view?
- What excuses might you need to overcome to achieve ownership?
- How can you move to be more open to the condition of others?

What Are Some Issues We Need to "Own" in Our Leadership?

Here are some issues to allow mercy to lead you into ownership:

- The grievous disunity in the church along racial lines.
- The limited knowledge of what the church is doing in your city across the ethnic spectrum.
- The enormous opportunity and economic gaps for communities of color.

- The United States is now the incarceration capital of the world.[1] When we fail to invest in the early years of vulnerable young people, the societal consequences are incomprehensible.
- A thirst for justice among young people is perhaps the most attractive dimension of the gospel for their generation.

Agency

Agency is when theory stops and action begins. In my (Claude's) devotion on Esther, we looked at how she used her agency as queen to affect legislation that would preserve her people. In some contexts, the only solution to massive inequities is legislative.

Wilson Goode grew up in North Carolina as a sharecropper. He worked in the fields from the age of six to fifteen. Growing up, Wilson experienced separation from his father when his dad spent some time in prison as the result of an altercation with his landlord after the landlord struck Wilson's mother. The pain he experienced through that separation gave him a profound awareness and sense of mercy for children of prisoners. "When I was separated from my dad when he was in prison, I realized Jesus' greatest pain on the cross was being separated from His Father."

Even after Wilson later moved to Philadelphia and became the first African American elected as mayor of that city, he never forgot his childhood experience. When he finished his second term, he went to work for the Department of Education as deputy assistant in charge of regional offices. He met John Dilulio, who was serving on the board of Public Private Ventures (PPV). PPV was committed to bringing about resources to challenging issues in cities. John wanted Wilson to identify Philadelphia churches that would provide mentors for children of prisoners.

Not only did Wilson identify the churches, he recruited

forty-two of them. Out of this effort Wilson developed the Amachi program, which provided mentors one hour a week for one year. The word *amachi* means, in Nigerian, "who knows what God has brought us through this child." Over the course of his leadership with Amachi, Wilson and the team recruited three hundred fifty thousand mentors for children of prisoners. Wilson used his agency as a former mayor and as an ordained Baptist clergy to engage the church of Philadelphia and the nation. Amachi was then soon established in all fifty states. Wilson has also been a core member of our Movement Day Philadelphia team.

Another person pursuing agency is Bob and Leslie Doll. Bob began as an investor in Movement.org in 2011 and joined the board in 2013, becoming its chair in 2016. He also serves as board chair of Lausanne to advance change for the good of the gospel in cities all around the globe.

Bob and Leslie have used their incredible agency to influence marketplace Christians toward consequential engagement. Leslie travels to the Middle East up to six times a year to encourage and support the work of indigenous Christians there. She partners with the work of Strategic Resource Group (SRG) in advancing the gospel in creative ways. SRG is a partnership of thirty-five Christian families impacting twenty-two nations in the Middle East. Her passion is rooted in helping the gospel grow in that part of the world. She is a voice for the persecuted and suffering church. And Bob has joined Khary Bridgewater as an advisor (see chapter 11). He uses his expertise to assist communities of need to become economically viable.

Philanthropically, Bob and Leslie have been investing in causes to address local needs in urban communities. For instance, they have been involved with the Sunday Breakfast Club in Philadelphia. In addition, their family volunteers at a local Thanksgiving service outreach. They model for us agency at a practical, local level.

And one more example is Doug Birdsall. As he was considering engaging evangelical Christians in civil dialogue around matters of consequence, Dylan Roof murdered nine people in Mother Emanuel Church. This was a point of profound awakening for Doug. Having owned the moment, he moved to personal, practical, and positional agency by leveraging his considerable relational capital to convene a racially diverse group of leaders in Washington, DC, to absorb, process, and consider what might be some next steps. For many, it was the first time being in a room with one another. Out of that meeting came more consultations in DC, as well as Atlanta, Boston, Chicago, and Los Angeles, culminating in Charleston on the one-year anniversary of the shooting. Those meetings resulted in some lasting connections and in launching several other initiatives.

While the heart of our book has concentrated on a United States context, these themes are universally significant. One of the great joys of my (Mac's) life has been to travel to Africa annually from 2002 to 2018. As mentioned earlier, I have taken 175 pastors to East Africa to see the work of World Vision. Spending time there has always been a great experience for my soul, given the vibrancy and joy of the African church.

Our first Movement Day gathering outside the United States was in Pretoria, South Africa, in 2015. South Africa has had its own unique and powerful racial struggles. Apartheid was the law of the land until 1994. Nelson Mandela was released from prison in 1990. I have seen his prison cell on Robbin Island. His story is one of great courage and endurance over the twenty-seven years he was imprisoned for seeking equality in that country.

Durban is one of the principal cities in South Africa, with the largest Indian population of any city outside of India. In Durban, an organization was birthed called City Story and has been a robust partner with Movement Day. Robert Ntuli and Peter

Watt are local pastors who have forged an important partnership through their work together.

Robert and Peter have led city-wide efforts to have racial conversations to address the rise of xenophobia in Durban and throughout the rest of South Africa. Many bordering countries have had refugees fleeing to South Africa because of its more mature economy. They have been a powerful portrait of African and Caucasian leaders working together to foster racial unity among the churches. They have brought their young people together in the hope that they will build lifelong biracial friendships. They have used their agency for good.

What Are Some Ways to Use Your Agency?

As we have discussed, agency is using our personal, practical, positional, political, and pecuniary (economic) agency. It is important that we think critically about how we do this.

With this in mind, here are some questions to ponder:

- How are you exercising your agency?
- Which category(s) are more challenging to exercise?
- How are you being challenged to stretch in the exercise of agency?
- What might help you exercise your agency?
- How will you exercise agency this week?

Need some ideas on where to start? Consider these:

- Build authentic relationships across racial lines. A litmus test of this reality in our lives is whether we share meals in the homes of those different from ourselves.
- Invest time in relationships. This means an ongoing deepening of relationships with the greatest of

intentions. God invites us to initiate toward others different from ourselves, to have a strategy of inclusion.

- Vote for change that advances the cause of a just society for the disadvantaged.
- Use your vocational influence and expertise to elevate the disenfranchised.
- Identify and invest in next-generation leaders who can make a difference (e.g., Marya and I [Mac] support Student Dream, an organization led by an African-American young woman that equips young African Americans to pursue entrepreneurship and wealth management).
- Organize a community of like-minded people interested in your own city and create an advisory board. Bring leaders together in a forum (like Movement Day) to define the challenges of the city and agencies that are collaborating to make a measurable difference.
- Become educated on the need for minority businesses in your city. Businesses need investment of capital and resources that can mature over time through the incubation and acceleration of a minority-owned business. Invest financially in causes and leaders that foster that work. Consider connecting with Inspire Equity (www.norstelcapital.com or www.inspireequity.com) or a similar organization. Just as the Good Samaritan had to invest financial resources to meet the needs of the injured Jewish person, so we must find strategic ways to invest financial resources to create opportunity for those who have less resources than we do.
- It is important for White evangelical pastors to know that other White evangelicals or White pastors are dealing with the issues of race. So connect with each other

so you can encourage each other and know that you are not alone. It isn't enough for a White pastor to be in relationship with a Black pastor. It is important for that White pastor to know that other White pastors are willing to take risks and get involved. It is pretty lonely if you feel as though you're a lone voice and you're out on a limb by yourself. So make those connections.

- Form alliances. Alliances always precede movements. Like the 757 (see chapter 7). As of this writing, they just had their seventieth consecutive call. And that is a biracial group who have been meeting every week since the end of February 2020. They've experienced a tremendous time of learning. That group would walk on nails for one another, because they have been together. People can say the hard things, but the others don't misinterpret them. If they need clarification, the group works at it. They have intentionally developed a depth of loyalty and bonding to one another that will give everybody that courage to do the right thing.

Now Go and Do Likewise

There is value in the Esther-Nehemiah-Ezra three-legged stool of how you affect change. Sometimes it is political. Sometimes it is mobilization. Sometimes it is spiritual. However you feel God calling you, now is the time to get to work. Just think: perhaps you are exactly where God placed you for such a time and for such a purpose as this.

Our greatest prayer and hope for you is that, in God's unique and generous way, He will arrest you and will continue to arrest all of us into these uncomfortable spaces. It is one thing to think and read about this topic. It is quite another to draw near and become part of the solution.

Now go and do likewise.

Jesus, You came as the Great Disruptor, and in Your own ownership and agency, You did the impossible. You transcended what we deserved and, instead of giving us justice, You gave us redemption. Your undeserved love and sacrifice tipped the scales forever on the side of mercy. We acknowledge that vast numbers of persons precious to You have not fully experienced justice or redemption. You invite us to be Christ figures and, in fact, to be Good Samaritans in our own cities and communities. Give us the courage, initiative, and intention to care for the bruised and beaten. Give us the perseverance to stay with those who have been mistreated. Allow us to live long enough to see the satisfaction of suffering alleviated and opportunity won for those who have been denied opportunity. We do this because of gratitude for Your intervention in our lives and for the sake of the world You love so much that You sacrificed all. Amen.

AFTERWORD

You just finished reading a book by two honest and courageous men who have sought to step into a volatile topic to launch a much-needed conversation among God's people.

They shared their personal stories. They've given us practical examples of other believers who started small and over time made a huge difference in their sphere of influence with regard to the racial divide. They helped us see what "the church" can actually do in a relatively short amount of time when commitment replaces platitudes, and pastors and leaders engage together as Black and White brothers and sisters in Christ to solve real problems in the name of Jesus.

But this book is not just about their stories or the progress made by others. We learned that we all need to be educated beyond our biases; we need proximity so that we can stop talking about "them" who do not look like us and start talking with them who are different from us. Change happens when we build an honest and real relationship with those who are not like us; it means entering their world, inviting them into ours, hearing their story, and seeing them first and foremost as brothers and sisters in Christ, not members of another race.

We all agree with that intellectually, but this book is a call to turning that belief into actual behaviors, actually reading, listening, learning, serving, and building an authentic relationship with a brother or sister in Christ whose story, background, and perspective is far different from ours.

The days of having a meeting, sharing a worship service, or doing photo ops of Whites and Blacks together in the name of Christ that don't get translated into real life relationships, meeting one another's needs, and refusing to be polarized by the media has to come to an end.

I am deeply aware that we all may not agree with certain portions of this book. As a White evangelical pastor who has taught on racism, modeled much of what is written in this book, and led a multicultural church, I felt a few twinges of resentment as I read some pages that seem to categorize me as biased just because I am White. I didn't like being lumped in with everyone else. The inner voice in my mind said, *But I'm not like that*, and then I realized that's how most all of us have been viewing this topic for years.

In a moment of honest reflection, I realized that I have a bias—a lens through which I look at every topic, not just racism. And it's imperfect; it's shaped by my background, by my worldview, my family, and my experiences both good and bad. Like you, I'm a fallen, imperfect human being. My perspective is not "the truth," and I don't see things accurately, objectively, or biblically 100 percent of the time. None of us do. But I want to learn, I want to grow, I want to see life and *all people* from Jesus' perspective. I want to let God change me, help me to be less defensive and less insecure as I take to heart His command to "make every effort to keep the unity of the Spirit through the bond of peace" (Ephesians 4:3) as it relates to my part in racial reconciliation and genuine partnership in the body of Christ.

It would be easy to focus on the parts of this book that you disagree with rather than actually applying the things that would make a difference in your life, your family, your church, and your community. So let's own where we have blown it, and commit to starting where we are, and moving to wherever God would take us. Let's stop talking and start acting on what we know is true, right, just, and godly. Here are some practical ways to get you started:

Confession: Pray, "Lord, show me my blind spots."

Education: Broaden your perspective on racism.

Proximity: Get to know someone different from you.

Forgiveness: "Clothe yourselves with compassion, kindness, humility, gentleness and patience. Bear with each other and forgive one another if any of you has a grievance against someone. Forgive as the Lord forgave you" (Colossians 3:12–13).

Resources: Carve out some time and money; get some skin in the game to actually make a difference.

Leadership: Use your influence, actions, and words to bring light not heat.

Cultures don't change by merely posting things on the internet, making great declarations that everyone should follow, or getting angry about what's not right. Cultures change one person at a time; it happens when others see you and me doing good, speaking differently, acting differently, and refusing to allow a political party, a news outlet, or the internet define our views.

Our good works and good words will be noticed. In time, they will follow our example. Good is more powerful than evil. So we need not wait for some messiah figure to make racism go away tomorrow. The Messiah has already come; we just need to follow Him, and the time is now!

—*Chip Ingram, founder, teaching pastor,*
and CEO of Living on the Edge

ACKNOWLEDGMENTS

We want to acknowledge the tremendous gift of Ginger Kolbaba to this book project, both as an editor and as a friend. Her effort, joy, and commitment have been extraordinary.

Thanks to David Sluka for his publishing consultation and assistance. Thanks to Marya Pier for helping us coordinate book distribution. Thanks to Christy Distler for her fantastic copyediting.

Thanks to The Park Church and Movement.org for their unwavering commitment to us in our leadership.

NOTES

Introduction: Addressing the Very Real Racial Tension

1 "Race Relations," Gallup, accessed July 14, 2021, https://news.gallup.com/poll/1687/race-relations.aspx.

2 "InterVarsity Research: Christian Student Attitudes Amid the COVID-19 Pandemic," InterVarsity and Pinkston, July 2021, https://pinkston.co/2021-Student-Survey.

3 David Kinnaman, "Barna's Perspective on Race and the Church," Barna, June 17, 2020, https://www.barna.com/barnas-perspective-on-race-and-the-church/.

4 "Race and the Church," Barna, accessed July 14, 2021, https://www.barna.com/raceandthechurch/#contentSection5.

Chapter 1: Origins in Black and White: Claude's Story

1 Michael E. Ruane, "Fifty Years Ago Some Called D.C. 'The Colored Man's Paradise.' Then Paradise Erupted," *Washington Post*, March 26, 2018, https://www.washingtonpost.com/local/fifty-years-ago-some-called-dc-the-colored-mans-paradise-then-paradise-erupted/2018/03/22/6ae9ec1c-208e-11e8-94da-ebf9d112159c_story.html.

2 Charles Stuart committed suicide a little more than two months later, on January 4, 1990.

3 Community Building Initiative, "About Us," accessed May 6, 2021, https://cbicharlotte.org/about-us/.

Chapter 2: Origins in Black and White: Mac's Story

1 For more information on the breakdown of the different Sioux tribes, please see "Need to Know: South Dakota Tribes," Native Governance Center, https://nativegov.org/south-dakota-tribes/.

2 Michael Trinkley, "South Carolina—African-Americans—Slave Population," South Carolina's Information Highway, accessed May 19, 2021, https://www.sciway.net/afam/slavery/population.html.

3 "Williamsburg County, South Carolina," Data USA, accessed May 19, 2021, https://datausa.io/profile/geo/williamsburg-county-sc#:~:text=The%205%20largest%20ethnic%20groups,(Hispanic)%20(0.764%25).

4   "Bernhard Goetz," *Biography*, May 12, 2020, https://www.biography.com/crime
    -figure/bernhard-goetz.

5   "25 Years in 25 Days (1990): NYC's Murder Rate Peaks," *The Brian Lehrer Show*,
    September 29, 2014, https://www.wnyc.org/story/25-years-25-days-1990-nycs
    -murder-rate-peaks/.

6   Dr. Jeffrey Burkes, NYPD Dental Forensics, as quoted in *The Power of a City at
    Prayer* (Downers Grove, IL: InterVarsity, 2002), 35.

7   Mona Charen, "Crime and Racism in New York City," *Chicago Tribune*, Sep-
    tember 17, 1990, https://www.chicagotribune.com/news/ct-xpm-1990-09-17
    -9003180114-story.html.

Chapter 3: An Invitation to a Racial Conversation

1   Quoted the Charlotte Chamber report, Raj Chetty, "Where Is the Land of
    Opportunity? The Geography of Intergenerational Mobility in the United
    States," 2015, 4.

Chapter 4: The Consistent Requirement

1   Martin Luther King Jr., "I Have a Dream," delivered August 29, 1963, at the
    Lincoln Memorial, Washington, DC, accessed June 14, 2021, https://www.
    americanrhetoric.com/speeches/mlkihaveadream.htm.

2   Ibid.

3   Julia Jackson, August 25, 2020, YouTube, https://www.youtube.com/watch?
    v=V-wj-BM0BOc.

4   Michael P. Green, in *1,500 Illustrations for Biblical Preaching* (Grand Rapids,
    MI: Baker, 2000), 208.

5   Charles Tindley, "Beams of Heaven," 1905, public domain.

Chapter 5: Coming to Terms

1   John A. Powell and Stephen Menendian, "The Problem of Othering: Towards
    Inclusiveness and Belonging," *Othering & Belonging*, issue 1, Summer 2016,
    https://otheringandbelonging.org/the-problem-of-othering/.

Chapter 6: A Necessary Conversation

1   *Race: The Power of an Illusion,* April 2003, www.racepowerofanillusion.org.

2   Gilder Lehrman Institute, "The Three-Fifth Compromise," Digital History ID
    163, accessed June 24, 2021, www.digitalhistory.uh.edu.

3   "Go Deeper: Race Timeline," *Race: The Power of an Illusion*, April 2003, https://
    www.pbs.org/race/000_About/002_03_d-godeeper.htm.

4   Al Bates, "Arizona History: The Path to Statehood: When Arizona Became a
    United States Territory," *Associated Press News*, April 15, 2019, https://apnews.
    com/article/224920232a414a638efa0399ac68a269.

5   Greg Nokes, "Black Exclusion Laws in Oregon," July 6, 2020, https://www.ore-gonencyclopedia.org/articles/exclusion_laws/#.YNTQJ-hKiUk.

6   "People v. Hall, 4 Cal. 399 (1854)," Caselaw Access Project, accessed June 24, 2021, https://cite.case.law/cal/4/399/.

7   "A Long History of Racial Preferences—for Whites," *Race: The Power of an Illusion*, April 2003, https://www.pbs.org/race/000_About/002_04-background-03-02.htm.

8   Henry Louis Gates Jr., "What Is Juneteenth?," PBS, June 16, 2013, https://www.pbs.org/wnet/african-americans-many-rivers-to-cross/history/what-is-juneteenth/.

9   "Slavery in the Choctaw and Chickasaw Nations," Access Genealogy, accessed June 24, 2021, https://accessgenealogy.com/oklahoma/slavery-in-the-choctaw-and-chickasaw-nations.htm.

10   David Pilgrim, "What Was Jim Crow?," Ferris State University, Jim Crow Museum of Racist Memorabilia, September 2000, revised 2012, https://www.ferris.edu/jimcrow/what.htm.

11   Hyung Kyu Nam, "Just an Environment or a Just Environment? Racial Segregation and Its Impacts," *Race: The Power of an Illusion*, April 2003, https://www.pbs.org/race/000_About/002_04-teachers-02.htm.

12   Erin Blakemore, "How the GI Bill's Promise Was Denied to a Million Black WWII Veterans," History, April 20, 2021, https://www.history.com/news/gi-bill-black-wwii-veterans-benefits.

13   "Brown v. Board of Education (1954)," Our Documents, accessed June 24, 2021, https://www.ourdocuments.gov/doc.php?flash=false&doc=87.

14   Jody Feder, "Federal Civil Rights Statutes: A Primer," Congressional Research Service, Report for Congress, March 26, 2012, https://www.llsdc.org/assets/sourcebook/crs-rl33386.pdf.

15   David Bailey, *Beyond Diversity: What the Future of Racial Justice Will Require of U.S. Churches,* April 27, 2021 https://www.barna.com/beyond-diversity/

Chapter 7: Movement Day 757: From Awareness to Transformation

1   "Norfolk's Affordable Housing Crisis and the Closure of the St. Paul's Public Housing Communities," Legal Aid Society of Eastern Virginia, accessed June 21, 2021, https://www.laseva.org/node/37/norfolks-affordable-housing-crisis-and-closure-st-pauls-public-housing-communities.

2   The Virginian-Pilot and Daily Press Editorial Board, "Editorial: An Alarming Snapshot of Hunger in Hampton Roads," *The Virginian-Pilot*, October 20, 2020, https://www.pilotonline.com/opinion/vp-ed-editorial-food-insecurity-1021-20201020-jqfde6dhmrhd5aj35mqbfain7a-story.html.

3   "2019 National Report Card," National Center for Educational Statistics, nces.ed.gov.

4   "Williamsburg-James City County Public Schools: National Assess-ment of Educational Progress (NAEP)," Virginia Department of Education, accessed June 24, 2021, https://schoolquality.virginia.gov/divisions/williamsburg-james -city-county-public-schools#desktopTabs-2.

5   Donald J. Hernandez, "Double Jeopardy: How Third-Grade Reading Skills and Poverty Influence High School Graduation," Annie E. Casey Foundation, Janu-ary 1, 2012, https://www.aecf.org/resources/double-jeopardy.

6   Andrew Sum, Ishwar Khatiwada, Joseph McLaughlin, et al, "The Consequences of Dropping Out of High School," Center for Labor Market Studies, North-eastern University, October 2009, https://www.prisonpolicy.org/scans/The _Consequences_of_Dropping_Out_of_High_School.pdf.

7   John Perkins is the Moses of the racial reconciliation movement and was named Mississippi's Man of the Century. He birthed the Christian Commu-nity Development Association, which has inspired and trained urban ministry practitioners for the past thirty years.

8   Don Roberts, WAVY.com, September 24, 2020, https://www.wavy.com/news/ local-news/newport-news/handshakes-conversation-and-bags-of-food-po-lice-building-relationships-with-residents-of-aqueduct-apartments/.

Chapter 8: Beyond Sympathy to Ownership

1   G. Curtis Jones, "Personal Involvement," *1,000 Illustrations for Preaching and Teaching* (Nashville, TN: B&H, 1986), 79, https://biblia.com/books/1000 illsprchtch/Page.p_79.

Chapter 9: One Race: Jack Alexander's Journey into Mercy

1   My (Claude's) appearance at Venture Christian Church came out of its pastor, Chip Ingram, taking ownership and inviting me to speak there. Being taken by the tweets and postings during the 2016 election cycle, Chip decided to dedicate several weekends of worship to addressing the topics of race, Islam, and women. Under the theme "Understanding: Know It Before You Post It," he invited people he believed would be able to address them. I was given the trust to address "Understanding Racism."

2   Gracie Bonds Staples, "Can We Allow What Has Broken the Heart of God to Break Ours?," *Atlanta Journal-Constitution*, August 12, 2019, https://www.ajc.com/ lifestyles/religion/can-allow-what-has-broken-the-heart-god-break-ours/ scHRic90g1FT2IbzQHNqhL/.

Chapter 10: Exercising Agency

1   Albert Bandura, "Agency," accessed June 22, 2021, https://albertbandura.com/ albert-bandura-agency.html.

2 Maggie Potapchuk, "Profile 3: Charlotte, North Carolina: Creating 'Eye to Eye' Leadership and Decision Making," *Community Change Processes in Addressing Racial Inequities*, Aspen Institute, October 2007, https://www.aspeninstitute. org/wp-content/uploads/files/content/docs/rcc/CMTYCHANGEPROCESS-REQUITYFINAL2.PDF.

3 Jennifer Billock, "How Moonshine Bootlegging Gave Rise to NASCAR," *Smithsonian* magazine, February 10, 2017, https://www.smithsonianmag.com/travel/how-moonshine-bootlegging-gave-rise-nascar-180962014/.

4 Juliet Macur, "Bubba Wallace Thankful for Flag Ban, but NASCAR's Fans Might Not Be," *New York Times*, June 22, 2020, https://www.nytimes.com/2020/06/13/sports/bubba-wallace-nascar-confederate-flag.html.

5 Charlotte Clergy and Community Leaders, "A Message for Our Black Neighbors," *Charlotte Observer*, June 8, 2020, https://www.charlotteobserver.com/opinion/article243180156.html

Chapter 11: Creating Opportunity: Khary Bridgewater's Mission to Inspire Equity

1 Michael Sasso, "Black Business Owners' Ranks Collapse by 41 Percent in US Lockdowns," *Bloomberg News*, June 8, 2020, https://www.bloomberg.com/news/articles/2020-06-08/black-business-owners-suffer-41-drop-in-covid-19-lockdowns.

2 Anthony Braga, David Kennedy, Elin Waring, et al., "Problem-Oriented Policing, Deterrence, and Youth Violence: An Evaluation of Boston's Operation Ceasefire," *Journal of Research in Crime and Delinquency*, vol 38, 3, August 2001, 195–226, https://journals.sagepub.com/doi/10.1177/0022427801038003001.

3 Larissa Borofsky, Ilana Kellerman, Brian Baucom, et al., "Community Violence Exposure and Adolescents' School Engagement and Academic Achievement Over Time," *Psychol Violence*, 3(4), October 1, 2013, 381–395, doi: 10.1037/a0034121.

4 Alyssa S. Parpia, Isabel Martinez, Abdulrahman M. El-Sayed, et al., "Racial Disparities in COVID-19 Mortality Across Michigan, United States," Elsevier, February 26, 2021, https://www.thelancet.com/pdfs/journals/eclinm/PIIS2589-5370(21)00041-9.pdf.

Chapter 12: Elephants and the Unfinished Task

1 Elena Aronson, "Discipling toward Racial Justice: A Q&A with Elena Aronson," The Barna Group, April 27, 2021, www.barna.com.

Chapter 13: What's Next?

1 "Highest to Lowest—Prison Population Total," World Prison Brief, 2016, https://prisonstudies.org/highest-to-lowest/prison-population-total?field_region_taxonomy_tid=All.

ABOUT THE AUTHORS

Bishop Claude Alexander has served as the senior pastor of The Park Church in Charlotte, North Carolina, for more than thirty years and is one of the most respected voices around the globe on the subject of race. He is a past president of the Hampton University Ministers Conference, the oldest and largest interdenominational gathering of African-American clergy in the United States. He serves on the boards of Charlotte Center City Partners, Christianity Today, Council for Christian Colleges and Universities, InterVarsity Christian Fellowship, BioLogos, and Movement.Org. He is the chair of Gordon-Conwell Theological Seminary board of trustees and the vice presiding bishop of the Kingdom Association of Covenant Pastors. Claude and his wife, Dr. Kimberly Nash Alexander, are the proud parents of two daughters, Camryn Rene and Carsyn Richelle.

Dr. Mac Pier is the founder of Movement.org and a Lausanne co-catalyst for cities. He has lived in New York City for more than thirty-five years where he founded the Concerts of Prayer Movement and cofounded Movement Day with Tim Keller. Movement Day has engaged leaders from six continents and nine hundred cities. Mac was a thirty-year resident of Flushing, Queens, a community with one hundred language groups. He has built multiracial, multilingual alliances around the globe. He and his wife, Marya, have three children (Anna, Jordan, and Kirsten) and three in-law children from Brazil, the Philippines, and India (Lucas, Christine, and Basanth), along with five grandchildren (Noah, Gabriel, Layla, Hayley, and Lily).